I0797827

The Vegan Kitchen

The Vegan Kitchen

Jean-Christian Jury

Φ

GLUTEN-FREE

NUT-FREE

5 INGREDIENTS OR FEWER

30 MINUTES OR LESS

ONE-POT

Introduction

In recent years, vegan cuisine has emerged as one of the world's most vibrant food movements. At the forefront of this renaissance was acclaimed French vegan and raw-food chef Jean-Christian Jury, a leading authority on plant-based cooking. Known for his encyclopaedic knowledge of vegan food traditions worldwide, Jury helped to transform the food world's perception of what vegan food can be—exciting, nourishing, and deeply satisfying.

This new selection of 75 of the finest vegan recipes from around the world is an essential companion for home cooks. Drawing on culinary global traditions, these dishes celebrate the diversity and abundance of plant-based ingredients in their own right. From comforting staples to vibrant street food, each recipe reflects Jury's belief that vegan cookery can be every bit as rich, varied, and rewarding as any other form of cuisine.

At the core is a total respect for ingredients. Without relying on dairy, eggs, or meat, it is the thoughtful layering of spices, herbs, textures, and natural sweetness or acidity that leads to each dish's success. In this collection, you'll find dishes built around legumes, whole grains, seasonal vegetables, nuts, seeds, and fermented foods, with influences ranging from the Middle East and East Asia to Africa, Latin America, and Europe. Whether it's a smoky aubergine dip, a fragrant vegetable curry, or a stew with warming spices, the emphasis is on bold, clean tastes and healthy, satisfying meals.

Jean-Christian Jury long advocated for an approach to vegan cooking that was rooted in cultural tradition rather than trend. Many of the world's oldest and most celebrated cuisines have their roots in plant-based recipes, whether as a result of the seasonality or scarcity of ingredients, or for reasons of religious practice. While celebrating those origins, the recipes in this new collection are all perfectly attuned to modern kitchens and tastes. You'll find recipes that require minimal equipment and straightforward techniques, making it possible to bring global vegan flavors to your table with ease.

With Jean-Christian Jury's global perspective and the authenticity and practicality of its recipes, *The Vegan Kitchen* offers an inspiring and practical guide for anyone looking to embrace plant-based eating—whether full-time or just a few meals at a time. These are dishes designed to satisfy, to share, and to celebrate the incredible variety the plant world has to offer. Cooked with care and curiosity, vegan food is never a compromise, but a revelation.

Starters

Eggplant and Tahini Meza

Armenia

⬠

Serves 4
Preparation time 30 minutes (including cooling)
Cooking time 1 hour

2 **eggplants** (aubergines), cut into thick slices

⅓ cup (75 g / 3 oz) **tahini**

3 tablespoons fresh **lemon juice**

2 tablespoons **olive oil**, plus extra to serve

2 **garlic cloves**, crushed

salt and freshly ground **black pepper**

2 tablespoons chopped **fresh parsley**, to garnish

crackers, to serve

Preheat the oven to 400°F/200°C/Gas Mark 6.

Place the eggplants (aubergines) in a baking pan and bake for 1 hour, until very soft. Let cool for 20 minutes, then discard the skins.

Transfer the eggplant flesh to a large bowl and mash with a fork. Add the tahini, lemon juice, olive oil, and garlic. Season to taste with salt and freshly ground black pepper, and mash the mixture with a fork (alternatively, blend using a food processor).

Transfer to a bowl, garnish with chopped parsley, drizzle with olive oil, and serve with crackers.

Colcannon

Ireland

Serves 4
Preparation time 20 minutes
Cooking time around 50 minutes

¼ cup (60 g / 2 oz) **vegetable margarine**, plus extra for brushing

1¾ lb (800 g) **russet potatoes** or similar, cut into medium-size chunks

salt and freshly ground **black pepper**

½ cup (120 ml / 4 fl oz) **soy cream**

1 cup (240 g / 8½ oz) **kale** or **curly kale**, cut into strips

1 **garlic clove**, finely chopped

green salad, to serve

French dressing, to serve

Preheat the oven to 350°F/180°C/Gas Mark 4. Grease a deep ovenproof dish with vegetable margarine.

Meanwhile, put the potato chunks into a saucepan of salted water and bring to a boil. Boil the potatoes for about 15 minutes, until very tender. Drain the potatoes, return them to the pan, and add half the vegetable margarine on top. Leave to melt, then mix well and mash the potatoes with a fork. Stir in the soy cream and season to taste with salt and freshly ground black pepper. Set aside.

Bring a saucepan of water to a boil, add the kale, and blanch over high heat for 3 minutes. Drain in a strainer (sieve).

Heat the remaining vegetable margarine in a skillet (frying pan), add the garlic, and stir-fry gently over medium heat for about 2–3 minutes, until it starts to brown. Add the kale and toss carefully.

Arrange alternating layers of mashed potato and kale in the prepared ovenproof dish, starting with kale and finishing with mashed potato. Transfer to the oven and bake for 30 minutes, until lightly browned on top. Garnish with a pinch each of salt and pepper. Serve with a lightly dressed green salad.

Chickpea Patties

Syria

⬠

Serves 4
Preparation time 1 hour 30 minutes (including chilling)
Cooking time 15 minutes

- 2 cups (350 g / 12 oz) cooked **chickpeas**, drained
- 1 **onion**, finely chopped
- 2 tablespoons chopped **fresh parsley**
- 2 tablespoons chopped **fresh mint**
- 1 tablespoon **bread crumbs**
- 1 **slice of bread**, soaked in soy milk
- ½ cup (60 g / 2 oz) **all-purpose (plain) flour**, plus extra for rolling
- **salt** and freshly ground **black pepper**
- **vegetable oil**, for deep-frying
- your favorite **dipping sauce**, to serve

Using a food processor or high-speed blender, pulse the chickpeas, onion, parsley, mint, breadcrumbs, bread, flour, and salt and freshly ground black pepper to taste until well mixed. Transfer to a bowl and refrigerate for 1 hour.

Begin to heat enough oil to deep-fry the patties in a deep saucepan or deep-fat fryer. Dust a plate or tray with flour. Line another plate with paper towels.

Using your hands, form the mixture into small patties. Roll these in the flour. When the oil is hot, carefully slide the patties into it and fry for 7–8 minutes, until golden brown on both sides. Drain with a slotted spoon and transfer to the paper towel–lined plate to absorb excess oil. Serve with your favorite dipping sauce.

Daikon Rolls with Avocado and Micro Greens

Japan

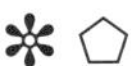

Serves 4
Preparation time 35 minutes

1 tablespoon **tamari** or **soy sauce**
1 tablespoon **rice vinegar**
1 tablespoon grated **galangal**
juice of 1 **lemon**
1 large **daikon radish**, sliced thinly into 12 long strips
12 **shiso leaves**
1 ripe **avocado**, finely diced
1 **cucumber**, finely diced
1 tablespoon **snow pea (mangetout) shoots**, minced
1 tablespoon chopped **fresh mint leaves**
black sesame seeds, to garnish
2 tablespoons **yuzu juice**

In a bowl, whisk together the tamari or soy sauce, rice vinegar, galangal, and lemon juice and set aside.

Lay out the daikon sheets on a tray or work surface. Place 1 shiso leaf on each daikon sheet.

Mix the avocado, cucumber, snow pea (mangetout) shoots, and mint together in a bowl. Stir in the lemon dressing. Divide the mixture equally among the daikon sheets, positioning the mixture at one end of each length. Roll up each daikon sheet tightly, pushing the roll away from you. Transfer the rolls to a serving plate, garnish with the black sesame seeds, and use a tablespoon to sprinkle the yuzu juice over the top.

Garden Spring Rolls

Vietnam

Serves 4
Preparation time around 45 minutes

½ pound (225 g / 8 oz) **rice vermicelli**

1 cup (125 g / 4¼ oz) **mung bean sprouts**

½ cup (120 g / 4 oz) grated **carrot**

½ cup (120 g / 4 oz) grated **daikon radish**

1 **garlic clove**, minced

1 tablespoon **tamari** or **soy sauce**

4 tablespoons **roasted unsalted peanuts**, crushed

¼ cup (30 g / 1 oz) **fresh mint**, chopped

¼ cup (30 g / 1 oz) **fresh cilantro** (coriander), chopped

1 tablespoon fresh **lime juice**

12 sheets of **rice paper**

1 tablespoon **sriracha**

Soak the rice vermicelli in hot water for 5 minutes, until soft. Drain, immerse in cold water, then drain again. Cut the noodles into 2-inch (5 cm) lengths and set aside.

Put the sprouts, carrot, daikon, garlic, and tamari or soy sauce into a large bowl and mix well. Add the vermicelli, then add half of the crushed peanuts, the mint, and the cilantro (coriander), and sprinkle with the lime juice. Toss together until combined.

Put some warm water into a large, shallow bowl. Immerse 1 sheet of rice paper in the water, quickly remove it, and lay the wrapper on a plate. Place about 2 tablespoons of the noodle mixture toward one end of the wrapper. Fold that end up over the mixture and roll it tightly to form a tube. Place the roll on a tray and cover with a clean, damp kitchen towel. Repeat with the remaining rice paper sheets and filling mixture.

Mix the sriracha with the remaining crushed peanuts and serve alongside the rolls.

Kimchi-Fried Rice

South Korea

Serves 4
Preparation time 20 minutes
Cooking time around 10 minutes

2 cups (300 g / 10½ oz) **vegan kimchi**

1 tablespoon **vegetable oil**

1 tablespoon toasted **sesame oil**

1 tablespoon **Korean gochujang** (fermented chili paste)

4 tablespoons **coconut cream**

4 cups (920 g / 2 lb) cooked **jasmine** or **short-grain rice**

3 **scallions** (spring onions), finely sliced

1 tablespoon **tamari** or **soy sauce**

1 tablespoon toasted **sesame seeds**, to garnish

4 sheets of **nori**, toasted and crumbled, to garnish

Drain the vegan kimchi in a colander set over a bowl, pressing to get as much juice out as possible. Reserve the juice. Chop the kimchi and set aside.

Heat the oils in a wok or skillet (frying pan), add the kimchi, and stir-fry gently for about 4–5 minutes over medium heat, until fragrant. Add the gochujang and coconut cream and toss for about 1 minute, until well blended. Add the rice, reserved kimchi juice, scallions (spring onions), and tamari or soy sauce, mix well, and continue to stir-fry for 3–4 minutes over medium heat, allowing the rice to lightly toast. Transfer to a serving plate and sprinkle with sesame seeds and nori crumbles. Serve immediately.

Portobello Carpaccio with Orange Tartare

Australia

Serves 4
Preparation time 20 minutes
Cooking time around 5 minutes

4 **portobello mushrooms**, stems and gills removed

2 tablespoons **olive oil**, plus extra for brushing

salt and freshly ground **black pepper**

2 **oranges**

½ cup (120 g / 4 oz) **black Kalamata olives**, pitted (stoned) and sliced

2 teaspoons **capers**, crushed

1 **shallot**, chopped

2 tablespoons **fresh cilantro** (coriander), chopped, to garnish

Preheat the broiler (grill). Line a baking sheet with aluminum foil.

Using a pastry brush, grease the mushrooms caps with olive oil and season to taste with salt and freshly ground black pepper. Arrange the mushrooms on the prepared baking sheet with the open sides facing upward. Set aside.

Grate the orange zest and set aside. Peel the oranges and separate the segments. Using a small knife, remove and discard as much of the fibers as possible, then chop the pulp. Transfer the chopped pulp to a bowl and mix in 1 teaspoon of the reserved orange zest along with the olives, capers, shallot, and olive oil. Season to taste with salt and freshly ground black pepper. Fill the mushroom caps with the mixture.

Broil (grill) the mushrooms at mid-height for 4–5 minutes. Transfer to serving plates, garnish with chopped cilantro (coriander), and serve immediately.

Raw Nori and Vegetable Rolls

The Netherlands

Serves 4
Preparation time 40 minutes

1 cup (150 g / 5 oz) **sunflower seeds**, soaked in water overnight

4 **scallions** (spring onions), chopped

¼ cup (20 g / ¾ oz) **fresh cilantro** (coriander)

4 tablespoons fresh **lemon juice**

2 **garlic cloves**, finely chopped

1 tablespoon **tamari** or **soy sauce**

½ cup (50 g / 1¾ oz) **cauliflower florets**

8 **romaine (cos) lettuce leaves**

8 sheets raw **nori**

1 **carrot**, peeled and julienned

1 **avocado**, halved, stoned, and thinly sliced

1 **cucumber**, peeled, seeded, and julienned

1 tablespoon **black sesame seeds**, to garnish

½ cup (40 g / 1½ oz) **microgreens** or **sprouts**, to garnish

soy sauce, to serve

wasabi, to serve

Rinse and drain the soaked sunflower seeds.

Using a food processor or high-speed blender, blend the sunflower seeds with the scallions (spring onions), cilantro (coriander), lemon juice, garlic, tamari or soy sauce, and 3 tablespoons water. Process until the mixture is very smooth. Transfer to a large bowl and set aside.

Now put the cauliflower florets into the bowl of the food processor or high-speed blender and pulse just until the cauliflower has the consistency of rice. Transfer to the bowl with the sunflower seed mixture and mix well.

Place 1 romaine lettuce leaf on a nori sheet, covering half the sheet. Spread 2 tablespoons of the sunflower seed–cauliflower mixture on the lettuce leaf. Divide the carrot, avocado, and cucumber strips into 8 portions and arrange one portion over the sunflower seed–cauliflower mixture. Fold the nori sheet over the filling and roll the sheet away from you as tightly as possible. Using your finger, wet the end of the nori sheet, then close and seal the roll. Repeat with the remaining nori sheets, lettuce leaves, and filling.

Using a very sharp knife, cut each roll into 4 or 6 pieces. Arrange the rolls on a serving plate. Sprinkle with black sesame seeds and garnish with microgreens or sprouts. Serve with soy sauce and wasabi on the side.

Stuffed Zucchini with Vegetables and Cheese

Moldova

Serves 4
Preparation time 30 minutes
Cooking time 30 minutes

- 4 **zucchini** (courgettes)
- 4 tablespoons **olive oil**
- 1 **celery stalk**, finely chopped
- ½ cup (120 g / 4 oz) sliced **carrots**
- 1 **onion**, chopped
- 2 plum **tomatoes**, diced
- **salt** and freshly ground **black pepper**
- 1 cup (240 g / 8½ oz) **tomato sauce**
- 1 cup (260 g / 9 oz) crumbled **vegan feta cheese**
- chopped **parsley**, to garnish (optional)

Preheat the oven to 400°F/200°C/Gas Mark 6.

Slice the zucchini (courgettes) in half lengthwise and scoop out the white flesh, leaving the shells intact. Reserve the flesh.

Heat 2 tablespoons of the olive oil in a skillet (frying pan) over medium heat, add the zucchini flesh, celery, carrots, onion, and tomatoes, and gently fry for 7–8 minutes. Season to taste with salt and freshly ground black pepper. Stuff the zucchini shells with the vegetable filling.

Pour the tomato sauce into an ovenproof dish. Arrange the zucchini boats in the dish. Top with the crumbled feta cheese and sprinkle over the remaining olive oil. Bake for 20 minutes. Garnish with chopped parsley to serve, if desired.

Salads

Chickpea and Cilantro Salad

Kurdistan

Serves 4
Preparation time 20 minutes
Cooking time 15 minutes

3 tablespoons **olive oil**

3 **garlic cloves**, finely chopped

1 **red onion**, finely chopped

1 tablespoon **ground cumin**

1 tablespoon finely chopped **fresh ginger**

½ teaspoon chopped **piment d'espelette**

2 tablespoons fresh **lime juice**

9 oz (250 g) plum **tomatoes**, quartered

1¼ cups (250 g / 9 oz) canned **chickpeas**, rinsed and drained

salt and freshly ground **black pepper**

1 bunch of **fresh cilantro** (coriander), chopped

Heat the oil in a wok or deep saucepan over medium heat. Add the garlic and onion and stir-fry for 5–6 minutes, until golden brown. Add the cumin, mix to incorporate, and fry for another 2 minutes. Now add the ginger, chili, lime juice, tomatoes, and chickpeas, reduce the heat to low, and simmer for 7–8 minutes.

Season to taste with salt and freshly ground black pepper, then transfer to a large serving bowl. Sprinkle with the chopped cilantro (coriander) and serve immediately.

Cucumber Relish

South Korea

Serves 4
Preparation time 40 minutes (including chilling)

3 **cucumbers**, peeled and thinly sliced on a mandoline

4 **garlic cloves**, finely chopped

5 **scallions** (spring onions), white parts only, finely chopped

4 tablespoons **tamari** or **soy sauce**

4 tablespoons **white vinegar**

1 tablespoon **sesame oil**

1 teaspoon **gochugaru** (Korean red chili powder)

steamed **jasmine** or **basmati rice**, to serve

Put the cucumber ribbons into a large bowl. Add the garlic and scallions (spring onions). Set aside.

Pour the tamari or soy sauce, white vinegar, and sesame oil into a small jar. Add the gochugaru, and whisk well. Dress the vegetables, refrigerate for 30 minutes, and serve with rice.

Chili-Mango Bowl

Guadeloupe

Serves 4
Preparation time 40 minutes (including chilling)

3 ripe **mangos**, peeled and sliced

1 **green apple**, peeled, cored, and diced

1 **fennel bulb**, trimmed and finely chopped

2 tablespoons minced **fresh mint**

1 **red onion**, finely chopped

1 tablespoon grated **fresh ginger**

juice of 2 **limes**

1 tablespoon **agave syrup**

1 **jalapeño pepper**, seeded and finely chopped

salt and freshly ground **black pepper**

Put the mangos, apple, fennel, mint, onion, and ginger into a large bowl. Sprinkle over the lime juice, add the agave syrup, and stir well to combine. Now sprinkle over the jalapeños and season to taste with salt and freshly ground black pepper. Refrigerate for 30 minutes before serving.

Red Bean Salad

Ecuador

Serves 4
Preparation time 12 hours 20 minutes (including chilling)

¼ cup (60 g / 2 oz) **tomato purée** (passata)

juice of 1 **lime**

4 tablespoons **olive oil**

1 tablespoon **white wine vinegar**

1 tablespoon **Dijon mustard**

1 teaspoon **superfine (caster) sugar**

salt and freshly ground **black pepper**

1 lb 2 oz (500 g) canned **red** or **kidney beans**, drained

1 **green bell pepper**, seeded and finely diced

1 **red bell pepper**, seeded and finely diced

1 **red onion**, finely chopped

1 cup (170 g / 6 oz) cooked **basmati** or other **long-grain rice**

1 tablespoon chopped **fresh cilantro** (coriander), to garnish

FOR THE VEGANNAISE

¾ cup (180 g / 6½ oz) **silken tofu**

4 tablespoons **vegetable oil**

juice of 1 **lemon**

1 teaspoon **onion powder**

1 tablespoon **white vinegar**

1 teaspoon **Dijon mustard**

For the vegannaise, use a food processor or blender to combine all the ingredients, processing for 2–3 minutes. Set aside in the refrigerator, where it will keep for 1 week.

Put the tomato purée (passata), lime juice, oil, vinegar, mustard, sugar, and 1 tablespoon vegannaise into a large bowl, season to taste with salt and freshly ground black pepper, and whisk until creamy. Add the red beans, bell peppers, and onion to the bowl and toss to mix. Refrigerate overnight.

To serve, stir in the rice, mix well, and garnish with chopped cilantro (coriander).

Roasted Couscous Salad with Vegetables

Israel

Serves 4
Preparation time 50 minutes (including standing)
Cooking time 10 minutes

FOR THE DRESSING

½ cup (120 ml / 4 fl oz) **balsamic vinegar**

1 teaspoon **Dijon mustard**

2 **garlic cloves**, finely chopped

½ cup (120 ml / 4 fl oz) **olive oil**

salt and freshly ground **black pepper**

FOR THE SALAD

1 **red bell pepper**, seeded and chopped

1 **yellow bell pepper**, seeded and chopped

2 **zucchini** (courgettes), quartered lengthwise and sliced

2 **summer squash**, quartered lengthwise and sliced

6 **asparagus spears**, trimmed and chopped

4 tablespoons **olive oil**

1 lb 2 oz (500 g) **medium-grain couscous**

2 cups (475 ml / 16 fl oz) **vegetable broth** (stock)

12 **cherry tomatoes**, halved

2 tablespoons chopped **fresh basil leaves**, to garnish

To make the dressing, put the vinegar, mustard, and garlic into a large jar and whisk, then slowly whisk in the olive oil until combined. Season to taste with salt and freshly ground black pepper and set aside.

To make the salad, mix the bell peppers, zucchini, summer squash, and asparagus in a large bowl. Pour over half the dressing, and toss to mix. Set aside for 30 minutes.

Heat 2 tablespoons of the olive oil in a skillet (frying pan), add the marinated vegetables, and cook over medium heat for 5–7 minutes, until tender. Transfer to a large bowl and set aside.

Heat the remaining olive oil in a saucepan over medium heat, add the couscous, and toast for about 3–4 minutes until lightly golden brown. Cover the couscous with the stock and bring to a boil, then remove the pan from the stove. Set aside, covered, until the couscous is al dente and almost all the stock has been absorbed.

Fluff the grains of couscous with a fork, then transfer to the bowl containing the vegetables. Add the tomatoes and the remaining dressing and mix well. Serve at room temperature, garnished with the chopped basil.

Soups

Black Bean and Mango Soup

Brazil

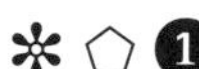

Serves 4
Preparation time 20 minutes
Cooking time 25 minutes

1 tablespoon **vegetable oil**

1 large **onion**, chopped

2 **garlic cloves**, minced

2 medium **sweet potatoes**, peeled and diced

1 large **red bell pepper**, seeded and diced

½ cup (110 g / 3¾ oz) canned **plum tomatoes**

1 small hot **green chile**, chopped

1½ cups (350 ml / 12 fl oz) **vegetable broth** (stock)

1 cup (220 g / 7¾ oz) canned **black beans**, drained

salt and freshly ground **black pepper**

1 ripe **mango**, diced

¼ cup (12 g / ½ oz) chopped **fresh cilantro** (coriander), to garnish

Heat the oil in a large saucepan over medium heat. Add the onion and cook, stirring often, for about 5 minutes, until softened. Stir in the garlic and cook, stirring, for 3–4 minutes, until the onion and garlic are golden. Stir in the sweet potatoes, bell pepper, the tomatoes with their juice, the chile, and the stock. Bring to a boil, then reduce the heat to low, cover the pan, and simmer for 15 minutes, until the sweet potatoes are tender.

Stir in the beans and simmer gently, uncovered, until they are heated through. Season to taste with salt and freshly ground black pepper. Stir in the mango and cook until heated through, about 1 minute.

Ladle the soup into bowls, garnish with cilantro (coriander), and serve.

Cilantro Soup

Portugal

Serves 4
Preparation time 35 minutes (plus cooling)
Cooking time 40 minutes

2 tablespoons **olive oil**

2 **onions**, finely chopped

2 **garlic cloves**, finely chopped

2 **tomatoes**, finely chopped

3 **potatoes**, peeled and diced

1 teaspoon **sweet paprika**

3 cups (750 ml / 25 fl oz) **vegetable broth** (stock)

1 **green bell pepper**, halved and seeded

1 bunch of **fresh cilantro** (coriander), stems tied together with kitchen string

1 cup (225 g / 8 oz) **long-grain rice**

salt and freshly ground **black pepper**

Heat 1 tablespoon of the olive oil in a stockpot over medium heat. Add the onions and stir-fry gently for 5–6 minutes, until they are translucent. Add the garlic, tomatoes, and potatoes and continue to cook for 4–5 minutes, until the potatoes are tender but firm.

Sprinkle the paprika over the mixture, stir well, then add the stock, green bell pepper, and cilantro (coriander) and bring to a boil. Immediately reduce the heat to low and simmer for 15 minutes. Add the rice and cook for another 15 minutes, until the rice is tender. Take the pan off the heat. Remove and reserve the cilantro and green pepper. Cover the pan with a lid and let the soup cool for 15 minutes.

Meanwhile, separate the cilantro stems from the leaves and discard the stems. Using a food processor or high-speed blender, blend the green pepper and cilantro leaves until smooth. Add the remaining olive oil and season to taste with salt and freshly ground black pepper. Blend again for 1 minute to combine.

Ladle the soup into large bowls, top with the cilantro–green bell pepper coulis, and serve.

Matzo Ball Soup

Israel

Serves 4
Preparation time 12 hours 25 minutes (including chilling)
Cooking time 45 minutes

FOR THE MATZO BALLS

1 lb 2 oz (500 g) **silken tofu**

4 tablespoons **olive oil**

9 oz (250 g) **matzo meal**

2 tablespoons **nutritional yeast**

1 teaspoon **baking powder**

1 teaspoon **onion powder**

1 teaspoon **garlic powder**

1 teaspoon **celery seeds**

salt and freshly ground **black pepper**

FOR THE SOUP

2 tablespoons **olive oil**

1 **onion**, chopped

2 **carrots**, sliced

2 **celery stalks**, chopped

2 tablespoons chopped **fresh dill**

6¼ cups (1.5 liters / 50 fl oz) **vegetable broth** (stock)

salt and freshly ground **black pepper**

2 tablespoons fresh **lemon juice**

2 tablespoons chopped **fresh parsley**, to garnish

To make the matzo ball dough using a food processor or high-speed blender, blend the tofu and olive oil. Transfer the mixture to a large bowl and stir in the matzo meal, nutritional yeast, baking powder, onion powder, garlic powder, and celery seeds. Season to taste with salt and freshly ground black pepper and stir well. Put the dough into an airtight container and refrigerate overnight.

For the soup, heat the olive oil in a large stockpot over medium heat. Add the onion, carrots, and celery and sauté for 5–6 minutes, until the onion is soft. Add the dill and stock, bring to a boil, then immediately reduce the heat to low and maintain a simmer.

Using your hands or a soup spoon, shape the dough into 2-inch (5 cm) balls. Carefully drop the dumplings into the soup, trying to not break them. Cover the pot and cook the soup at a low simmer for 40 minutes. Remove the pot from the heat, season the soup to taste with salt and freshly ground black pepper, and stir in the lemon juice. Garnish with the parsley and serve immediately.

Roasted Pumpkin and Red Lentil Soup

Turkey

Serves 4
Preparation time 35 minutes
Cooking time 1 hour

3 cups (710 ml / 24 fl oz) **vegetable broth** (stock)

1 cup (240 g / 8½ oz) **red lentils**, soaked in water overnight and drained

2 teaspoons **ground turmeric**

1¼ teaspoons **ground cumin**

1 tablespoon grated **fresh ginger**

1 teaspoon freshly ground **black pepper**, plus more as needed

1 teaspoon **salt**, plus more as needed

6 tablespoons **olive oil**

2¼ lb (1 kg) **Hokkaido pumpkin**, peeled and diced

1 **onion**, quartered

1 head of **garlic**, unpeeled

1 **lemon**, cut into 6 wedges

3 **fresh sage sprigs**, halved

¼ cup (6 g / ¼ oz) finely chopped **fresh parsley**

1 teaspoon **sweet paprika**

Preheat the oven to 440°F/230°C/Gas Mark 7½. Line a rimmed baking sheet with parchment (baking) paper.

Pour the stock into a large saucepan, add the lentils, and bring to a boil, then reduce the heat to medium and simmer for 30 minutes, until the lentils are tender.

Combine the turmeric, 1 teaspoon of the cumin, the ginger, 1 teaspoon freshly ground black pepper, salt, and 2 tablespoons of the olive oil in a large mixing bowl. Add the pumpkin and onion chunks and mix well to coat the vegetables in the spices. Transfer the pumpkin and onion to the prepared baking sheet and tuck the head of garlic and the lemon wedges in between the pumpkin and onion pieces. Arrange the sage around the pumpkin cubes. Bake for about 15 minutes, then remove the garlic and set aside. Return the other vegetables to the oven and bake for another 15 minutes.

Discard the sage and peel the baked garlic. Scrape the pulp from the lemon wedges, removing the seeds. Reserve the peel. Using a food processor or high-speed blender, blend the lentils with the garlic, lemon pulp, pumpkin, and onion in batches until smooth. Season to taste with salt and freshly ground black pepper.

Finely chop the reserved roasted lemon peel. Heat the remaining olive oil in a small saucepan over medium heat. Stir in the parsley, lemon peel, paprika, and the remaining cumin. As the spices release their aroma, remove the pan from the heat.

Ladle the soup into bowls, garnish with the spiced parsley and lemon peel, and serve.

Wild Mushroom and Potato Soup

Latvia

Serves 4
Preparation time 30 minutes
Cooking time 35 minutes

2 tablespoons **olive oil**

2 tablespoons **vegetable margarine**

1 lb 10½ oz (750 g) **wild mushrooms**, roughly chopped

4 tablespoons **dry white wine**

6 **russet potatoes**, diced

4 cups (960 ml / 32 fl oz) **vegetable broth** (stock)

2 tablespoons **vegetable oil**

1 **onion**, finely chopped

1 cup (240 g / 8½ oz) **smoked tofu**, diced

1 cup (240 ml / 8 fl oz) **soy cream**

1 teaspoon **sweet Hungarian paprika**

salt and freshly ground **black pepper**

4 tablespoons unsweetened **vegan Greek yogurt**, to garnish

2–3 **fresh dill sprigs**, fronds chopped, to garnish

Heat the olive oil and margarine in a stockpot over medium heat. Add the mushrooms and sauté for 5–6 minutes, stirring frequently. Add the white wine, stir to combine, then add the potatoes and stock and bring to a boil. Immediately reduce the heat to medium and simmer for about 15–20 minutes, until the potatoes are cooked. Using a slotted spoon, transfer three-quarters of the potatoes to a food processor or high-speed blender and purée until smooth. Return the puréed potatoes to the pot.

While the potatoes are cooking, heat the vegetable oil in a saucepan over medium heat. Add the onion and tofu and stir fry gently for 7–8 minutes, until the tofu is golden brown on all sides. Add the onion-tofu mixture, soy cream, and paprika to the soup and stir to combine. Season to taste with salt and freshly ground black pepper. Ladle the soup into bowls, garnish with yogurt and dill, and serve.

Tofu and Rice Noodle Soup

China

Serves 4
Preparation time 20 minutes
Cooking time 10 minutes

1 lb 2 oz (500 g) **rice noodles**

3 cups (710 ml / 24 fl oz) **vegetable broth** (stock)

1 tablespoon grated **fresh ginger**

2 tablespoons **canola (rapeseed) oil**

3 **garlic cloves**, finely chopped

9 oz (250 g) **smoked tofu**, diced

1 lb 2 oz (500 g) **baby bok choy**, trimmed

2 teaspoons **toasted sesame oil**, to garnish

1 cup (35 g / 1¼ oz) **bean sprouts**, to garnish

Cook the rice noodles according to the packet instructions. Rinse under cold water, drain, and set aside.

Pour the stock into a large pot, add the ginger, and bring to a boil. Reduce the heat to low and simmer for 5 minutes. Set aside.

Heat the canola (rapeseed) oil in a skillet (frying pan) over medium heat, add the garlic, and stir-fry gently for 2 minutes, until light golden. Remove the skillet from the heat and set aside.

Return the stock to a boil over medium heat. Add the smoked tofu and baby bok choy and cook for 2–3 minutes. Add the noodles and bring to a boil.

Ladle the soup into bowls, garnish with sesame oil, the fried garlic, and sprouts, and serve.

Main Courses

Carrot and Pea Curry

India

Serves 4
Preparation time 20 minutes
Cooking time 25 minutes

2 tablespoons **olive oil**

4 **curry leaves**

1 tablespoon crushed **red chili flakes**

1 teaspoon **mustard seeds**

1 tablespoon finely chopped **fresh ginger**

1 cup (240 g / 8½ oz) sliced **carrots**

2 cups (280 g / 9¾ oz) frozen **green peas**

2 teaspoons **yellow curry powder**

1 teaspoon **ground turmeric**

salt and freshly ground **black pepper**

2 cups (275 ml / 16 fl oz) **vegetable broth** (stock)

chopped **fresh cilantro** (coriander), to garnish

chopped **green chilies**, to garnish

chapati, to serve

Heat the oil in a skillet (frying pan) over medium heat. Add the curry leaves, then the crushed red chili flakes, mustard seeds, and ginger and stir-fry for 2 minutes. Add the carrots, peas, curry powder, and turmeric and cook for 3–4 minutes. Season to taste with salt and freshly ground black pepper.

Add the stock and simmer over medium heat for about 15 minutes, until the liquid has reduced by half. Garnish with cilantro (coriander) and green chilies and serve with chapati.

Potato Masala

Suriname

Serves 4
Preparation time 20 minutes
Cooking time 25 minutes

2 tablespoons **sunflower or corn oil**

1 **onion**, diced

2 **garlic cloves**, finely chopped

1 tablespoon **garam masala**

1 lb 2 oz (500 g) **potatoes**, quartered

about 3½ cups (870 ml / 28 fl oz) **coconut milk**

1 lb (450 g) canned **chickpeas**, drained

salt and freshly ground **black pepper**

cooked **basmati** or **jasmine rice**, to serve

In a large skillet (frying pan) over medium heat, warm the oil, add the onion and garlic, and cook, stirring, for about 4–5 minutes, until golden brown.

Add the garam masala to the pan and stir to coat the onion and garlic with it. Immediately add the potatoes and enough coconut milk to cover the potatoes. Cook over medium heat for about 15 minutes, until the potatoes are tender. Add the chickpeas, reduce the heat to low, and simmer for 3–4 minutes.

Season to taste with salt and freshly ground black pepper and serve with basmati or jasmine rice.

LA COCOTTE
STAUB
STAUB

Fruit Curry with Peanuts

Rwanda

Serves 4
Preparation time 30 minutes
Cooking time 20 minutes

2 tablespoons **vegetable oil**

2½ cups (350 g / 12 oz) peeled, cored, and chopped **tart apples** such as Granny Smith

1 cup (140 g / 5 oz) chopped **yellow onion**

2 teaspoons **curry powder**

1½ cups (120 g / 4 oz) **raisins**

1½ cups (120 g / 4 oz) chopped **dried apricots**

½ cup (60 g / 2 oz) **roasted peanuts**

salt and freshly ground **black pepper**

sticky, **Arborio**, or **Carnaroli rice** cooked in coconut milk, to serve

Heat the vegetable oil in a large skillet (frying pan) over medium heat. Add the apples and onion and sauté, stirring frequently, for 6–7 minutes, until the onion is translucent. Add the curry powder, 2 tablespoons water, the raisins, apricots, and peanuts, and season to taste with salt and freshly ground black pepper. Stir well to blend the ingredients together, then bring the mixture to a low simmer and cook for 12 minutes.

Serve warm or cold with sticky, Arborio, or Carnaroli rice cooked in coconut milk.

Artichokes with Almonds and Fava Beans

Spain

Serves 4
Preparation time 45 minutes
Cooking time 35 minutes

2 tablespoons fresh **lemon juice**, plus juice of 1 **lemon**

4 large **globe artichokes**

2 tablespoons **olive oil**

2 cups (480 g / 1 lb 1 oz) **fava (broad) beans**, shelled and cooked

1 cup (140 g / 5 oz) toasted **almonds**

½ cup (30 g / 1 oz) chopped **fresh dill**

salt and freshly ground **black pepper**

1 (14 oz / 400 g) can chopped **tomatoes**

Fill a large bowl with cold water and add 2 tablespoons of lemon juice. Trim the stalks off each artichoke, pull off all the leaves, and reserve the meatiest ones. Using a teaspoon, dig out the choke and cut out the bases to make a neat cup. Drop the cups into the acidulated water and set aside until ready to cook.

Drain the artichoke cups and transfer them to a medium sauté pan.

In a small bowl, combine the oil, remaining lemon juice, and 4 tablespoons of water and pour the mixture over the artichokes in the pan. Set the pan over medium heat, cover with a lid, and poach the artichokes for 20 minutes, until fork-tender but firm.

Add the fava (broad) beans and almonds to the pan, cover again with the lid, and cook for another 10 minutes. Add half of the dill and season to taste with salt and freshly ground black pepper. Transfer the mixture to a platter.

Put the tomatoes into the same sauté pan and bring to a simmer over medium heat. Return the artichokes, fava beans, and almonds to the pan, reduce the heat to low, and cook for 10 minutes. Season to taste with salt and freshly ground black pepper, if needed.

Meanwhile, bring a saucepan of salted water to a boil and cook the reserved artichoke leaves for about 12 minutes, until tender, then drain.

Transfer the artichoke mixture to a platter and garnish the plate by surrounding the artichoke mixture with the leaves, like a flower, if desired. Garnish with the remaining dill.

Baked Tofu with Tomato Rice

Bahamas

Serves 4
Preparation time 2 hours 15 minutes (including compressing)
Cooking time 45 minutes

1 lb 2 oz (500 g) **firm tofu**, sliced 1 inch (2.5 cm) thick

a generous 2 cups (500 ml / 17 fl oz) **tomato sauce**

2 tablespoons fresh **lime juice**

1 tablespoon finely chopped **onion**

1 teaspoon **dried oregano**

½ teaspoon **garlic powder**

salt and freshly ground **black pepper**

vegetable oil or **cooking spray**, for greasing

2 tablespoons **coconut powder**

fresh basil, to garnish

cooked **white basmati** or other **long-grain rice**, to serve

Place the tofu in a strainer (sieve), place the strainer in a clean sink, then place a weight, such as a cast-iron saucepan, over them and leave for 1–2 hours to squeeze out the water and compress the tofu.

Meanwhile, combine the tomato sauce, lime juice, onion, oregano, and garlic powder in a bowl and season to taste with salt and freshly ground black pepper. Set aside.

Preheat the oven to 350°F/180°C/Gas Mark 4. Lightly oil a 7 × 11-inch (18 × 28-cm) baking pan, or spray pan with a nonstick cooking spray.

Spoon about a third of the sauce into the prepared pan. Place the tofu slices on top and pour over the remaining sauce. Sprinkle over the coconut powder. Bake for 45 minutes.

Garnish with the basil and serve with rice.

Banana Blossom in Coconut Cream

Philippines

Serves 4
Preparation time 1 hour 30 minutes (including chilling)
Cooking time 20 minutes

2 **banana blossoms** (fresh or canned)

2 tablespoons **salt**, plus extra to season

2 tablespoons **vegetable oil**

2 **garlic cloves**, finely chopped

2 **yellow onions**, sliced

1 cup (200 g / 7 oz) sliced **tomatoes**

2 dried **red chilies**, crushed

2 tablespoons **white vinegar** mixed with 4 tablespoons **water**

freshly ground **black pepper**

1 cup (240 ml / 8 fl oz) **coconut milk**

cooked **long-grain** or **wild rice**, to serve

If using fresh banana blossoms, remove the first couple of leaves. Thinly slice the blossoms crosswise and place the slices in a bowl. Add 2 tablespoons salt, mix well, and refrigerate for 1 hour. Rinse under cold water and squeeze to dry. Set aside.

Heat the oil in a large skillet (frying pan) over medium heat. Add the garlic and cook, stirring, for about 2 minutes, until light brown. Add the onions and cook, stirring, for about 5–6 minutes, until translucent, then add the tomato slices and chilies and cook for about 3 minutes, until soft.

Add the banana blossoms and vinegar-water mixture to the vegetables and, without stirring, bring to a vigorous simmer. Cook for about 3 minutes, season to taste with salt and freshly ground black pepper, and stir. Continue to cook until the banana blossoms are tender, about 5–6 minutes. Add the coconut milk and remove the skillet from the heat. Let the mixture stand for a few minutes to allow the flavors to develop.

Serve with long-grain or wild rice on the side.

Beet Borani

Azerbaijan

Serves 4
Preparation time 4 hours (including chilling)
Cooking time 40 minutes

kosher salt and freshly ground **black pepper**

about 1½ lb (750 g) **beets** (beetroot), peeled, greens reserved

3 cups (720 g / 1 lb 9 oz) unsweetened **vegan Greek yogurt**

½ bunch **fresh dill**, finely chopped, plus extra to garnish

5 **fresh oregano sprigs**, leaves chopped

2 **garlic cloves**, crushed

2 cups (240 g / 8½ oz) toasted **pecans**

vegan naan, to serve

Fill a saucepan with salted water and bring to a boil over high heat. Add the beets (beetroot), reduce the heat to medium, and cook the beets, uncovered, for about 30–35 minutes, until tender.

Meanwhile, chop the beet greens. Wash but do not dry them. Put the greens into a sauté pan and set over high heat. Cover with a lid and steam in the water that remains on the leaves for 2–3 minutes, until wilted. Drain both the greens and the beets and let cool for 20 minutes.

Stir together the yogurt, dill, oregano, and garlic and season to taste with salt and freshly ground black pepper.

Cut the beets into medium slices and add them to the greens. Arrange them in a large bowl, alongside the yogurt dressing. Season to taste with salt and freshly ground black pepper. Cover the bowl with plastic wrap (clingfilm) and refrigerate for at least 3 hours. Sprinkle with the pecans and a little more dill, and serve with naan.

Braised Red Cabbage and Beets

Germany

Serves 4
Preparation time 45 minutes
Cooking time 1 hour 35 minutes

1 head of **red cabbage**, finely shredded

2 tablespoons **olive oil**

1 **onion**, thinly sliced

2 **garlic cloves**, crushed

3 **quinces**, peeled, cored, and cut into large slices

4 tablespoons **red wine vinegar**

1¼ cups (300 ml / 10 fl oz) **vegetable broth** (stock), plus more as needed

salt and freshly ground **black pepper**

3 **beets** (beetroot), peeled and grated

boiled or baked **potatoes**, to serve

Put the shredded cabbage into a Dutch oven (casserole).

Heat the oil in a skillet (frying pan) over medium heat. Add the onion and garlic and sauté for 5–6 minutes, until golden brown. Add the quince, vinegar, and broth and season to taste with salt and freshly ground black pepper. Cook for 5 minutes over medium heat, until the quince is fork-tender.

Transfer the mixture to the Dutch oven, stir to combine with the cabbage, cover with a lid and place the pot into an unheated oven. Set the oven temperature to 375°F/190°C/ Gas Mark 5 and cook for about 1 hour.

Stir in the beets (beetroot). Add extra stock if the vegetables seem a bit dry. Cover the pot and cook for another 25 minutes.

Serve hot, with potatoes.

Budapest Stew

Hungary

Serves 4
Preparation time 30 minutes
Cooking time 30 minutes

2 tablespoons **vegetable oil**

1 large **yellow onion**, chopped

1 lb 2 oz (500 g) **basmati** or other **long-grain rice**

a pinch of **salt**, plus extra to season

3 tablespoons sweet or hot **Hungarian paprika**

freshly ground **black pepper**

3 **yellow bell peppers**, chopped

3 sweet **red Romano peppers**, chopped

3 fresh **tomatoes**, diced, or ½ cup (115 g / 4 oz) tomato purée (passata)

chopped **fresh cilantro** (coriander) or **parsley**, to garnish

Heat the oil in a saucepan over medium heat. Add the onion and cook for 5–6 minutes, until golden brown. Remove one-third of the onion from the pan, transfer it to a large saucepan, and mix it with the rice. Set aside the pan containing the remaining onion.

Set the saucepan with the rice–onion mixture over medium heat and sauté for 2 minutes, stirring constantly. Cover with water, add a pinch of salt, and bring to a boil. Reduce the heat to medium-low, cover the pan with a lid, and cook for about 12–14 minutes, until the rice is soft but still al dente.

Place the pan containing the remaining onions on the stove. Add the paprika and mix well until it is dissolved. Add ½ cup (120 ml / 4 fl oz) cold water, season to taste with salt and freshly ground black pepper, then bring to a boil. Add the peppers and tomatoes or tomato purée (passata). Pour in enough water to cover the peppers and bring to a boil. Reduce the heat to low and simmer for 5 minutes.

Transfer the cooked rice to a serving plate, cover with the pepper sauce, and garnish with chopped cilantro (coriander) or parsley.

Caramelized Pineapple and Tofu

Cambodia

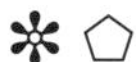

Preparation time 25 minutes
Cooking time 30 minutes
Serves 4

- 1½ cups (270 g / 9½ oz) chopped **pineapple**
- 1 lb 2 oz (500 g) **diced tofu**, fried
- 1 **garlic clove**, finely chopped
- 2 tablespoons **tamari** or **soy sauce**
- 1 tablespoon **superfine (caster) sugar**
- 2 **scallions** (spring onions), sliced
- **salt** and freshly ground **black pepper**
- 2 tablespoons chopped **fresh cilantro** (coriander), to garnish
- cooked **basmati** or other **long-grain rice**, to serve

Put the pineapple, tofu, garlic, tamari or soy sauce, and ½ cup (120 ml / 4 fl oz) water into a Dutch oven (casserole). Add the sugar and scallions (spring onions) and season to taste with salt and freshly ground black pepper. Stir well. Set the Dutch oven over medium heat and cook for about 30 minutes, until the liquid has reduced by half.

Transfer the stew to a serving dish, garnish with the cilantro (coriander), and serve over rice.

Caribbean Jerk Chili

Dominican Republic

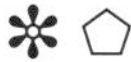

Serves 4
Preparation time 20 minutes
Cooking time 40 minutes

2 tablespoons **olive oil**

3 **garlic cloves**, finely chopped

2 **celery stalks**, diced

1 **onion**, diced

1 **red bell pepper**, diced

2 teaspoons **Jamaican jerk** seasoning or **chili sauce**

1 cup (240 ml / 8 fl oz) **coconut milk**

3 tablespoons **tomato purée** (passata)

1 cup (240 g / 8½ oz) canned **red** or **kidney beans**, drained

2 tablespoons fresh **lime juice**

salt and freshly ground **black pepper**

1 **mango**, diced

½ cup (30 g / 1 oz) chopped **fresh cilantro** (coriander)

cooked **basmati rice**, to serve

Heat the olive oil in a large saucepan over medium heat. Add the garlic, celery, onion, and bell pepper and sauté for 5–6 minutes, until the onion is translucent. Add the jerk seasoning or chili sauce and cook for 2–3 minutes. Stir in the coconut milk, tomato purée (passata), beans, and fresh lime juice and season to taste with salt and freshly ground black pepper, if needed. Cover the saucepan with a lid, reduce the heat to low, and simmer for 20 minutes, stirring occasionally.

Stir in half of the mango and half of the cilantro (coriander), then cover the saucepan and simmer for another 10 minutes. Serve the chili over rice, garnished with the remaining mango and cilantro.

Flambé Potatoes with Oyster Mushrooms

Cuba

Serves 4
Preparation time 35 minutes
Cooking time 1 hour 10 minutes

1 lb 2 oz (500 g) **fingerling potatoes**, halved

2 tablespoons **olive oil**

2 teaspoons **mixed dried herbs** of your choice

salt and freshly ground **black pepper**

1 **onion**, chopped

2 **garlic cloves**, finely chopped

2 **bay leaves**

9 oz (250 g) **oyster mushrooms**, sliced

1 cup (240 ml / 8 fl oz) **vegetable broth** (stock)

2 tablespoons light **rum**

chopped **fresh cilantro** (coriander), to garnish

Preheat the oven to 400°F/200°C/Gas Mark 6.

Arrange the potato halves on a rimmed baking sheet, brush with 1 tablespoon of the olive oil, sprinkle with mixed herbs, and season to taste with salt and freshly ground black pepper. Bake for 35–40 minutes, until soft. Transfer the potatoes to a skillet (frying pan) and set aside.

Heat the remaining olive oil in a large skillet over medium heat. Add the onion and stir-fry for 5–6 minutes, until soft and translucent. Add the garlic and bay leaves and stir-fry for 3–4 minutes, until lightly golden. Add the oyster mushrooms and stir-fry for 2–3 minutes. Pour in the stock, bring to a boil, then reduce the heat to low and simmer for 15 minutes, until the liquid has reduced by nearly half. Transfer the mixture to a large serving plate.

In a small saucepan over medium heat, bring the rum to a simmer, then pour it over the potatoes. Ignite the alcohol with a lighter and flambé for 2–3 minutes, until the flames die out.

Arrange the flambéed potatoes over the stew on the serving plate, garnish with chopped cilantro (coriander), and serve immediately.

Leeks in Mustard Sauce

Ireland

Serves 4
Preparation time 20 minutes
Cooking time 20 minutes

FOR THE VINAIGRETTE

4 tablespoons **olive oil**

3 tablespoons **red wine vinegar**

2 tablespoons **whole grain mustard**

2 **shallots**, finely chopped

FOR THE LEEKS

salt and freshly ground **black pepper**

6 **leeks**, white and pale green parts only

2 tablespoons chopped **fresh parsley**, to garnish

3 tablespoons chopped toasted **walnuts**, to garnish

baked potatoes or **boiled potatoes**, to serve

To make the vinaigrette, put the olive oil, vinegar, mustard, and shallots into a bowl and whisk together.

For the leeks, bring a large saucepan of salted water to a boil. Carefully drop in the leeks and simmer over medium heat for about 15 minutes, until tender and easily pierced with the tip of a knife. Drain the leeks and pat dry with paper towels. Slice the leeks in half lengthwise.

Arrange the leeks on a serving plate and pour over the vinaigrette. Garnish with parsley and walnuts and season to taste with salt and freshly ground black pepper. Serve with baked or boiled potatoes.

Miso-Glazed Eggplant

Japan

Serves 4
Preparation time 20 minutes
Cooking time 40 minutes

FOR THE GLAZE

4 tablespoons **yellow miso**

4 tablespoons **mirin**

4 tablespoons **sake**

2 tablespoons **superfine (caster) sugar**

FOR THE EGGPLANT

2 large **eggplants** (aubergines)

2 tablespoons **vegetable oil**

½ cup (120 ml / 4 fl oz) **sake**

½ cup (120 ml / 4 fl oz) **vegetable broth** (stock)

2 **scallions** (spring onions), finely chopped, to garnish

2 teaspoons grated **fresh ginger**, to garnish

To make the glaze, use a whisk to mash the ingredients together in a saucepan, ensuring there are no lumps of miso remaining. Bring the sauce to a boil over medium heat, then immediately reduce the heat to low and simmer, stirring constantly, for 8–9 minutes, until thick. Remove the pan from the stove, cover to keep warm, and set aside.

For the eggplant (aubergine), halve the eggplants lengthwise, then cut a cross-hatch pattern into the surface of the exposed flesh, ensuring the knife cuts about three-quarters of the way through the eggplant but does not cut through to the skin. (These cuts will help the glaze penetrate the eggplant during cooking.)

Heat the oil in a large sauté pan over medium heat. Fry the eggplant halves with the cut surfaces facing down for 6–7 minutes, until golden brown. Flip the eggplant halves over, then add the sake and immediately cover the pan to capture the steam. Cook, covered, for about 10 minutes, until the sake is reduced completely. Flip the eggplant halves back over, then add the stock. Cover with the lid and steam for about 15 minutes, until the tip of a knife passes through the eggplant easily. If the eggplants are still too hard, add a little water and continue to steam. Remove the lid to allow any excess water to evaporate.

Transfer the eggplants to a plate and brush with the glaze. Garnish with the chopped scallions (spring onions) and ginger and serve immediately.

Potato and Kalamata Olive Stew

Greece

Serves 4
Preparation time 30 minutes
Cooking time 45 minutes

4 tablespoons **olive oil**

1½ lb (680 g) **potatoes**, cut into wedges

8 **garlic cloves**, finely chopped

2 cups (280 g / 9¾ oz) **Kalamata olives**, pitted (stoned) and sliced

9 oz (250 g) **sundried tomatoes**, rehydrated and chopped

½ cup (120 ml / 4 fl oz) **dry white wine**

½ cup (120 ml / 4 fl oz) **vegetable broth** (stock)

1 tablespoon **dried oregano**

1 tablespoon **dried basil**

1 tablespoon **dried thyme**

salt and freshly ground **black pepper**

green salad, to serve

Heat the oil in a large skillet (frying pan) over medium heat. Add the potatoes and toss to coat. Add the garlic and cook for 3–4 minutes, until the garlic begins to turn golden. Add the olives and sundried tomatoes and stir well, then pour in the white wine and stock. Cover, reduce the heat to a low simmer, and cook for 30 minutes, until the potatoes are tender. Add the oregano, basil, and thyme and season to taste with salt and freshly ground black pepper. Stir well and simmer for another 10 minutes. Serve with a salad.

Squash with Prunes

Iran

Serves 4
Preparation time 30 minutes
Cooking time 35 minutes

3 tablespoons **olive oil**

1 teaspoon **ground cardamom**

1 teaspoon **ground cloves**

2 **onions**, sliced

2¼ lb (1 kg) **butternut squash**, peeled and cut into 2-inch (5 cm) dice

3 **garlic cloves**, finely chopped

2 tablespoons fresh **lime juice**

2 cups (480 g / 1 lb 1 oz) pitted (stoned) and chopped **prunes**

1½ cups (350 ml / 12 fl oz) **vegetable broth** (stock)

2 tablespoons chopped toasted **almonds**, to garnish

cooked **wild rice** or warm **vegan naan**, to serve

Heat the olive oil in a saucepan. Add the cardamom and ground cloves and cook over medium-high heat for about 1 minute, until fragrant, then add the onions and squash. Cook for about 15 minutes, until the onions are golden. Add the garlic, lime juice, prunes, and stock, bring to a boil, then reduce the heat to low and simmer for 15 minutes, until the butternut squash is tender.

Transfer to a serving plate, garnish with the chopped almonds, and serve with rice or naan.

Chickpea Curry Burritos with Mint and Chili Sauce

Mexico

Serves 4
Preparation time 35 minutes
Cooking time 50 minutes

FOR THE MINT AND CHILI SAUCE

2 teaspoons **granulated sugar**

1 teaspoon **salt**

1 tablespoon chopped **fresh ginger**

1 small **serrano** or **jalapeño pepper**, seeded and chopped

1 **garlic clove**, finely chopped

3 cups (75 g / 3 oz) **fresh mint**, chopped

2 tablespoons **rice vinegar** or **apple cider vinegar**

FOR THE BURRITOS

3 large **garlic cloves**, finely chopped

1 tablespoon finely chopped **fresh ginger**

1 **jalapeño pepper**, trimmed, seeded, and chopped

1 large **onion**, chopped

1 tablespoon **canola (rapeseed) oil**

1½ tablespoons **curry powder**

1 tablespoon **ground cumin**

1 lb 2 oz (500 g) **potatoes**, diced

½ cup (80 g / 3 oz) **currants** or **raisins**

salt

2 cups (280 g / 9¾ oz) canned **chickpeas**, drained

1 cup (240 g / 8½ oz) frozen **peas**, defrosted

½ cup (60 g / 2 oz) **fresh cilantro** (coriander), chopped

8 **flour tortillas**

To make the mint and chili sauce, first put the sugar and salt into the bowl of a high-speed blender or mini food processor. With the motor running, drop in the ginger, chili pepper, and garlic and process until finely chopped. Add the mint and vinegar. Pulse until everything is finely chopped, scraping down the sides of the bowl if needed. Transfer to a small serving bowl and refrigerate until ready to serve.

To make the burritos, use a food processor or high-speed blender to process the garlic, ginger, and jalapeño, pulsing until the mixture is reduced to a paste. Add the onion and pulse until it is coarsely chopped.

Heat the oil in a large nonstick skillet (frying pan). Add the onion mixture and stir-fry over medium heat, stirring constantly, for 5–6 minutes, until light golden. Add the curry powder and cumin and cook, stirring constantly, for about 2 minutes, until fragrant. Add the potatoes, 1½ cups (350 ml / 12 fl oz) water, and the currants or raisins and season to taste with salt. Bring to a simmer, then reduce the heat to low, cover the skillet with a lid, and simmer for about 30 minutes, until the potatoes are tender. Stir in the chickpeas, peas, and cilantro (coriander). Cook for about 3–4 minutes over medium heat and adjust the seasoning as necessary.

Meanwhile, gently heat the tortillas in a hot skillet. Wrap them in aluminum foil to keep them warm.

To serve, set out the warm tortillas on a plate, with the curry filling and the mint and chili sauce in separate bowls.

Soup Dumplings

China

Serves 4
Preparation time 35 minutes
Cooking time 1 hour 15 minutes

FOR THE DUMPLINGS

1 lb 2 oz (500 g) **russet potatoes** or similar

3 tablespoons **olive oil**

6 **onions**, chopped

9 oz (250 g) **shiitake mushroom caps**, chopped

9 oz (250 g) grated **vegan cheese**

1 bunch **fresh cilantro** (coriander), chopped

2 tablespoons **nutritional yeast**

salt and freshly ground **black pepper**

40 round or square **vegan wonton wrappers**

FOR THE SOUP

2 tablespoons **olive oil**

1 **onion**, chopped

2 **tomatoes**, chopped

1 tablespoon chopped **fresh cilantro** (coriander)

2 cups (480 ml / 16 fl oz) **vegetable broth** (stock)

chopped **scallions** (spring onions), to serve

soy sauce, to serve

To make the dumplings, put the potatoes into a saucepan and cover them with water. Bring to a boil and cook for 35–40 minutes, until the potatoes are fork-tender. Drain the potatoes, then using a food processor or high-speed blender, mash them until smooth. Set aside to cool.

Heat the olive oil in a saucepan. Add the onions and cook over medium heat for 5–6 minutes, until soft. Add the mushrooms, cover the pan, and cook for about 5 minutes, until the mushrooms are soft. Transfer the mixture to a bowl and let cool. Once cool, mix in the cooled potatoes, grated vegan cheese, chopped cilantro (coriander), and nutritional yeast and season to taste with salt and freshly ground black pepper.

Lay a wonton wrapper on a work surface. Place 1 tablespoon of the filling mixture on the wrapper, then fold the wrapper over the filling and press the edges together to seal. (Use the tines of a fork to press the edges to seal them effectively.) Set aside on a tray and repeat with the remaining wrappers and filling, but do not pile up the dumplings on the tray—keep them separate.

Fill a large steamer pan with water. Bring the water to a boil. Steam the dumplings in batches, arranging them in the steamer basket so that they are placed well apart—they will expand during cooking, so if they are too closely placed, they will stick together. Steam each batch for about 15 minutes, until the dumplings are firm.

To make the soup, heat the olive oil in a saucepan. Add the onion and cook over medium heat for 5–6 minutes, until soft. Add the tomatoes and chopped cilantro and cook for 5 minutes, then add the stock, bring to a simmer over medium heat, and cook for 4–5 minutes.

Ladle out the soup and divide the dumplings into bowls. Serve with the scallions (spring onions) and soy sauce on the side.

Karachi Dumplings

Pakistan

Serves 4
Preparation time 30 minutes
Cooking time 30 minutes

FOR THE DUMPLINGS

2 cups (200 g / 7 oz) **yellow lentil flour**

1½ teaspoons **baking soda** (bicarbonate of soda)

vegetable oil, for deep-frying

salt

FOR THE YOGURT SAUCE

1 lb 10½ oz (750 g) unsweetened **vegan yogurt**

2 teaspoons **superfine (caster) sugar**

1 teaspoon **salt**

2 tablespoons **garam masala**

To make the dumplings, combine the lentil flour, baking soda (bicarbonate of soda), and ½ cup (120 ml / 4 fl oz) water in a large bowl and mix well until smooth. Set aside for 20 minutes.

Heat enough oil in a wok, deep saucepan, or deep-fat fryer over medium heat to deep-fry the dumplings. Line a tray with paper towels. Carefully drop 1 tablespoon of the batter into the hot oil, and repeat for as many dumplings as will fit in the pan, reducing the heat to medium-low to avoid burning the dumplings. As soon as they become golden brown, 8–9 minutes, remove them from the oil with a slotted spoon and transfer to the paper-lined tray to absorb the excess oil. Repeat with the remaining batter. Let the cooked dumplings cool.

To make the yogurt sauce, use a food processor or blender to combine the yogurt with the sugar, salt, and garam masala.

Serve the dumplings at room temperature with the yogurt sauce on the side.

Hazelnut and Bean Burger

New Zealand

Serves 4
Preparation time 40 minutes
Cooking time 35 minutes

1½ cups (120 g / 4 oz) **hazelnuts** or **almonds**, crushed

1 cup (200 g / 7 oz) canned **tomatoes**

1½ cups (360 g / 12½ oz) cooked **kidney** or **pinto beans**

2 cups (240 g / 8½ oz) **bread crumbs**, plus extra as needed

1 tablespoon **tahini**

1 teaspoon **ground cumin**

2 tablespoons **nutritional yeast**

salt and freshly ground **black pepper**

TO SERVE

4 **burger buns**

your favorite burger **sauces**

tomato slices, to garnish

onion slices, to garnish

lettuce leaves, to garnish

dill pickles, to garnish

Preheat the oven to 375°F/190°C/Gas Mark 5.

Using a food processor or high-speed blender, process all the ingredients to a smooth purée.

Divide the mixture into 4 equal portions and form each into a patty. If the mixture is too wet, add more breadcrumbs. Transfer the patties to a baking sheet and bake for 35 minutes, until well cooked.

Split the burger buns. Spread a little of your favorite burger sauces on the bottom half of each bun, then place a burger on top. Top the burger with tomato slices, onion slices, lettuce leaves, and dill pickles, and cover with the top of the bun.

Corn Cake

Nicaragua

Serves 4
Preparation time 1 hour 45 minutes (including chilling)
Cooking time 1 hour 40 minutes

FOR THE CORN CAKE

4 cups (960 g / 2 lb 2 oz) **yellow cornmeal**

2½ cups (600 ml / 20 fl oz) fresh **orange juice**

salt

½ cup (120 ml / 4 fl oz) **coconut oil**

1 cup (240 ml / 8 fl oz) **olive oil**, plus extra for greasing

1–3 **banana leaves**

FOR THE FILLING

2 tablespoons **olive oil**

2 **onions**, chopped

2 **garlic cloves**, finely chopped

1 **red bell pepper**, chopped

4 **tomatoes**, diced

2 **potatoes** or **sweet potatoes**, peeled, boiled, and diced

1 cup (120 g / 4 oz) **corn kernels**, fresh or frozen

1 teaspoon **ground cumin**

1 teaspoon **sweet paprika**

1 teaspoon **cayenne pepper**

1 tablespoon **nutritional yeast**

1 bunch **fresh mint**, finely chopped

2 teaspoons **raisins**

1 cup (140 g / 5 oz) **Kalamata olives**, pitted (stoned) and sliced

3 tablespoons fresh **lemon juice**

freshly ground **black pepper**

green salad, to serve

French dressing, to serve

sriracha sauce, to serve

To make the corn cake dough, put the cornmeal and orange juice into the bowl of a food processor and season to taste with salt. Process to combine, then keep the motor running while you slowly add the oils. Process until the dough is smooth but firm.

Grease a large ovenproof dish with olive oil. Cover the bottom and sides with a banana leaf. Use 2 if necessary to cover the dish, overlapping each other—do not cut the leaves as you will need the overhanging parts to cover the dough.

To make the filling, heat the olive oil in a saucepan. Add the onions, garlic, and bell pepper and stir-fry for 5–6 minutes over medium heat, until the onions and garlic are golden brown. Transfer to a large bowl, mix in the remaining filling ingredients, and season to taste with salt and freshly ground black pepper.

Divide the dough into 4 portions. Spread out 1 portion of dough in a layer on the bottom of the prepared dish. Top this with one-third of the filling mixture. Add another layer of dough, then add a second layer of the filling, using half of the remaining mixture. Top this with another layer of dough, then add a final layer of the filling mixture. Top with the final portion of dough. Cover the dish with the overhanging banana leaves, adding 1 more leaf if necessary to cover the dough completely. Refrigerate for 1 hour.

Preheat the oven to 375°F/190°C/Gas Mark 5.

Transfer the dish to the oven and bake for 1 hour, then reduce the heat to 275°F/140°C/Gas Mark 1 and cook for another 30 minutes, until cooked through and browned on top. Let cool for 15 minutes.

Serve with a lightly dressed salad and sriracha sauce on the side.

Pizza with Lemons and Brussels Sprouts

Belgium

Serves 4
Preparation time 2 hours (including rising)
Cooking time 20 minutes

FOR THE DOUGH

1 packet (15 g / ½ oz) **dry active (fast-action) yeast**

2 tablespoons **agave syrup**

3 tablespoons **olive oil**, plus extra for brushing and greasing

1 teaspoon **salt**

1 cup (125 g / 4½ oz) **bread flour**, plus extra for dusting

1 cup (125 g / 4½ oz) unbleached **all-purpose (plain) flour**

FOR THE TOPPING

9 oz (250 g) **Brussels sprouts**, halved

1 **shallot**, finely chopped

1 **Meyer lemon**

9 oz (250 g) **vegan mozzarella cheese**

4 teaspoons **olive oil**

salt and freshly ground **black pepper**

To make the dough using a stand mixer with a dough hook attachment, combine ¾ cup (175 ml / 6 fl oz) warm water with the yeast and agave syrup until the yeast is dissolved. Set aside for 20 minutes to allow the yeast to become active. Add the oil, salt, and bread flour to the mixer bowl, then set the mixer to a low-speed setting and mix the ingredients for 7–8 minutes, scraping down the sides if needed, until the dough is smooth. With the motor running, add 2 tablespoons of the all-purpose flour at a time, in 2–3-minute intervals. After the final addition, when the dough starts to come together, mix for another 2–3 minutes, then transfer the dough to a large bowl, brush with olive oil, and cover with a clean kitchen towel. Set aside in a warm place for 1 hour and let rise.

To make the topping, using a food processor fitted with an S-blade, pulse the Brussels sprouts and shallot until nicely shredded. Set aside. Thinly slice the Meyer lemon, then cut each slice in 2, removing the seeds as needed. Set aside.

Preheat the broiler (grill) of your oven and arrange a rack in the upper-third section of the oven. Grease a baking sheet with olive oil.

Divide the dough into 4 equal portions and roll each portion into a ball in your hands. Roll out 1 portion into a circle roughly 10 inches (25 cm) in diameter. Transfer the dough to the prepared baking sheet. Sprinkle over a quarter of the Brussels sprout–shallot mix, then arrange a quarter of the Meyer lemon slices on the top. Finish with a quarter of the vegan mozzarella cheese. Bake for 3–4 minutes, watching closely to prevent the crust from burning. Repeat with the remaining pizza dough and ingredients. Drizzle 1 teaspoon of olive oil over each cooked pizza, season to taste with salt and freshly ground black pepper, and serve.

Portobello Bruschetta

United States

⬠

Serves 4
Preparation time 2 hours (including chilling)
Cooking time 10 minutes

FOR THE MARINATED MUSHROOMS

½ cup (120 ml / 4 fl oz) **olive oil**

4 tablespoons **balsamic vinegar**

2 **garlic cloves**, finely chopped

1 tablespoon **dried basil**

1 tablespoon **tamari** or **soy sauce**

4 large **portobello mushrooms**, trimmed

FOR THE BRUSCHETTA TOPPING

2 tablespoons **olive oil**

2 tablespoons **balsamic vinegar**

1 tablespoon **Dijon mustard**

1 tablespoon **vegannaise** (page 38) or use store-bought

salt and freshly ground **black pepper**

4½ oz (125 g) **cherry tomatoes**, diced

¼ **red bell pepper**, diced

2 **garlic cloves**, finely chopped

1 small **onion**, diced

1 tablespoon chopped **fresh basil**

1 **baguette**, halved crosswise

olive oil, for brushing

To make the mushrooms, put all the ingredients, except the mushrooms, into a large bowl and whisk together until well combined. Add the mushrooms to the marinade and toss to coat. Refrigerate for 1 hour.

Preheat the broiler (grill). Line a broiler pan with aluminum foil and arrange the mushrooms on top. Grill the mushrooms for 2–3 minutes on each side, until light golden brown. Let cool.

To make the bruschetta, put the olive oil, vinegar, mustard, and vegannaise into a large bowl, season to taste with salt and freshly ground black pepper, and whisk until smooth. Add the tomatoes, bell pepper, garlic, onion, and basil, toss the vegetables in the dressing, and refrigerate for 30 minutes.

Split each baguette in half lengthwise. Brush the insides of the bread with a little olive oil.

Dice the mushrooms. To serve, divide the mushrooms among the baguette pieces. Spoon the vegetables on top and serve.

Veggie Burgers

United States

Serves 4
Preparation time 1 hour 25 minutes (including chilling)
Cooking time 20 minutes

FOR THE BURGERS

1 cup (240 g / 8½ oz) white **short-grain rice**

1 cup (200 g / 7 oz) **Puy lentils**

2 tablespoons **vegetable oil**, plus extra for greasing

½ cup (120 g / 4 oz) **pecans**

1 **red onion**, finely chopped

1 **portobello mushroom**, finely chopped

1 cup (200 g / 7 oz) **cornstarch** (cornflour)

2 slices **sandwich bread**

½ cup (75 g / 3 oz) raw **sunflower seeds**, processed into a paste

1 handful of **fresh parsley**, chopped

1 teaspoon **baking powder**

1 teaspoon **chili powder**

1 teaspoon **curry powder**

½ cup (120 g / 4 oz) **silken tofu**

salt and freshly ground **black pepper**

TO ASSEMBLE

2 tablespoons **vegetable oil**

2 tablespoons each **tomato ketchup** and **Dijon mustard**

1 **portobello mushroom**, chopped

½ **onion**, sliced into rings

4 **burger buns**, split

Iceberg lettuce leaves, roughly chopped

¼ **cucumber**, sliced

2 **dill pickles**, sliced

2 tablespoons **vegannaise** (page 38) or use store-bought

4 slices **vegan cheese**

To make the burgers, cook the rice and lentils according to the packet instructions. Drain and set aside.

Grease a baking sheet with oil.

Using a food processor or high-speed blender, pulse the pecans to chop coarsely. Put them into a large bowl along with the red onion and mushroom and mix well. Add the cooked rice and lentils and the remaining ingredients, except the silken tofu, and mix well. Using a fork, mash the silken tofu to a purée and add to the mixture. Season to taste with salt and black pepper and stir until well combined. Divide the mixture into 4 equal portions and, with slightly wet hands, shape each portion into a tight round patty. Arrange the patties on the prepared baking sheet and freeze for 1 hour.

Heat 2 tablespoons vegetable oil in a large skillet (frying pan) over medium heat. Add the patties and fry gently for 6–7 minutes on each side, until golden brown on both sides.

Meanwhile, to assemble, heat the remaining oil in another large skillet (frying pan). Add the mushroom and onion rings and stir-fry for 7–8 minutes, until golden brown. Transfer to a bowl and set aside.

Put the burger buns in the same skillet, cut sides down, and toast for 2 minutes over medium-low heat.

Spread a little mustard on the bottom burger buns, then build your burger with the other ingredients as you prefer. Add the top half of the buns to complete, and serve immediately.

Crispy Orange-Ginger Tofu with Broccoli

China

Serves 4
Preparation time 2 hours 35 minutes (including draining)
Cooking time 45 minutes

1 lb 10½ oz (750 g) **extra-firm tofu**

1 cup (240 ml / 8 fl oz) fresh **orange juice**

⅓ cup (80 g / 3 oz) plus 1½ tablespoons **cornstarch** (cornflour)

2 tablespoons **light brown sugar**

1 tablespoon **tamari** or **soy sauce**

1 tablespoon grated **fresh ginger**

2 **garlic cloves**, finely chopped

1 tablespoon finely grated **orange zest**

2 tablespoons **vegetable oil**

1 large head of **broccoli**, broken into florets

cooked **basmati** or other **long-grain rice**, to serve

2 **scallions** (spring onions), finely chopped, to garnish

1 tablespoon **sesame seeds**, to garnish

1 tablespoon crushed **red chili flakes**, to garnish

Place the tofu in a clean sink and weigh it down with something heavy, such as a cast-iron saucepan, for 1–2 hours to squeeze out the water and compress the tofu.

Pour half of the orange juice into a bowl and stir in 1½ tablespoons of cornstarch (cornflour) until dissolved. Set aside.

Put the remaining orange juice into a small saucepan along with the brown sugar, tamari or soy sauce, ginger, garlic, and orange zest. Bring to a low simmer and cook over medium-low heat for about 15 minutes, until reduced by half.

Stir in the cornstarch mixture until completely blended. Remove the pan from the stove and set aside.

Cut the tofu into cubes and roll in the remaining cornstarch to coat.

Coat the bottom of a large skillet (frying pan) with the vegetable oil and set over medium-high heat. Add the tofu cubes and cook over medium heat for 5–6 minutes on each side, until browned and crispy. Transfer to a plate lined with paper towels to absorb excess oil.

Bring water to a boil in a steamer pan. Place the broccoli in the steamer basket and steam for about 20 minutes, or to your desired tenderness.

Return the tofu to the skillet along with the broccoli and sauce. Toss everything to coat.

Serve over rice, garnished with scallions (spring onions), sesame seeds, and crushed red chili flakes.

Stir-Fried Bok Choy with Tofu

Philippines

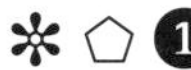

Serves 4
Preparation time 20 minutes
Cooking time 20 minutes

3 tablespoons **vegetable oil**

1 **onion**, chopped

3 **garlic cloves**, finely chopped

1 cup (240 g / 8½ oz) **diced tofu**

3 cups (270 g / 9½ oz) **baby bok choy**, chopped

1 cup (240 g / 8½ oz) diced **summer squash**

2 cups (260 g / 9 oz) diced **zucchini** (courgette)

1 cup (180 g / 6½ oz) **cherry tomatoes**, halved

2 tablespoons grated **fresh ginger**

1 tablespoon **tamari** or **soy sauce**

½ cup (120 ml / 4 fl oz) **vegetable broth** (stock)

1 tablespoon fresh **lime juice**

salt and freshly ground **black pepper**

chopped **fresh cilantro** (coriander), to garnish

cooked **white rice**, to serve

Heat 2 tablespoons of the oil in a wok. Add the onion and garlic and stir-fry over medium heat for 5–6 minutes, until golden. Add the tofu and stir-fry gently for 3–4 minutes over medium heat, until lightly browned. Add the bok choy, squash, zucchini (courgette), and tomatoes and stir-fry gently for 4–5 minutes. Remove the vegetables and tofu from the wok and set aside.

Heat the remaining oil in the same wok over medium heat. Add the ginger and tamari or soy sauce and cook for 1–2 minutes, until the tamari starts to simmer. Add the stock, bring to a boil, then reduce the heat to medium-low and simmer for about 10 minutes, until the liquid has reduced by half. Add the lime juice and season to taste with salt and freshly ground black pepper. Return the vegetables and tofu to the wok. Cook for 2 minutes, until fork-tender.

Garnish with cilantro (coriander) and serve immediately, with rice.

Grains & Beans

Butternut Squash and Sage Risotto

Italy

Serves 4
Preparation time 50 minutes (including cooling)
Cooking time 1 hour 15 minutes

3 tablespoons **olive oil**, plus extra for greasing

2 **butternut squash**, halved lengthwise, seeds and fibers removed

1 **shallot**, finely chopped

1½ cups (360 g / 12½ oz) **Arborio** or **Carnaroli rice**

2 cups (475 ml / 16 fl oz) **vegetable broth** (stock)

1 **orange**

salt and freshly ground **black/white pepper**

2 tablespoons **all-purpose (plain) flour**

1 handful of **fresh sage leaves**

1 tablespoon **vegetable margarine**

grated **vegan parmesan cheese**, to garnish

¼ cup (30 g / 1 oz) **pine nuts**, to garnish

Preheat the oven to 400°F/200°C/Gas Mark 6. Grease a baking pan with olive oil.

Arrange the butternut squash halves on the prepared baking pan with the cut sides facing down. Cover the pan with aluminum foil and bake for about 45 minutes, until fork-tender. Let cool for 20 minutes.

Heat the oil in a large skillet (frying pan) over medium heat. Add the shallot and stir-fry for 2 minutes, until golden. Add the rice and stir well to coat in the oil. Stir in 1 ladle of stock, then cook over very low heat until the stock has been absorbed. Immediately, add another ladle of stock, repeating until the rice is cooked but still al dente.

Meanwhile, cut the orange in half, juice the halves, and remove the white pith from the peel before cutting half of the peel into fine strips. Set aside.

Peel the cooked butternut squash, then finely dice it, and add the squash to the risotto along with the orange juice. Stir carefully until everything is nicely blended. Cook over very low heat for 3–4 minutes. Season to taste with salt and freshly ground black pepper.

Spread the flour on a plate and fill a small bowl with warm water. Dip the sage leaves, one at a time, into the warm water, then dip them into the flour to coat.

Melt the vegetable margarine in a saucepan. Add the flour-coated leaves and fry for a few seconds, until fragrant. Set aside.

Ladle the risotto into bowls and garnish with vegan cheese, strips of orange zest, the pine nuts, and the fried sage leaves.

Couscous Stew with Mushrooms

Israel

Serves 4
Preparation time 20 minutes
Cooking time 20 minutes

2 cups (475 ml / 16 fl oz) **vegetable broth** (stock)

2 tablespoons **olive oil**

1 lb 2 oz (500 g) **shiitake** or **portobello mushrooms**, sliced

1 **green chile**, seeded and finely chopped

2 **shallots**, finely chopped

2 **carrots**, diced

1 lb 2 oz (500 g) **medium-grain couscous**

9 oz (250 g) **green peas**

salt and freshly ground **black/ white pepper**

3 tablespoons chopped **fresh chives**

2 tablespoons chopped **fresh parsley**

sriracha or **harissa**, to serve

Bring the stock to a boil in a large saucepan. Reduce the heat to low and keep the stock simmering.

Heat 1 tablespoon of the olive oil in a large saucepan. Add the mushrooms and chile and sauté over medium heat for 5 minutes, until the mushrooms have released their juices. Drain with a slotted spoon and transfer to a bowl. Set aside.

Heat the remaining olive oil in the same saucepan over medium heat. Add the shallots and sauté for 2 minutes, until soft. Add the carrots and sauté for 4–5 minutes, then add the couscous and cook for 3 minutes, stirring constantly, until lightly browned. Stir ¼ cup (60 ml / 2 fl oz) of the stock into the mixture. Reduce the heat to low and add another ¼ cup (60 ml / 2 fl oz) of the stock. Repeat the process until all the stock has been absorbed by the couscous.

Stir the peas and the mushroom mixture into the saucepan and cook over medium heat for another 2 minutes, until the peas are hot. Season to taste with salt and freshly ground black pepper.

Transfer to a serving plate, sprinkle over the chives and parsley. Serve immediately, with sriracha or harissa on the side.

Quinoa Mathrooba

Bahrain

Serves 4
Preparation time 20 minutes
Cooking time 45 minutes

2½ cups (600 ml / 20 fl oz) **vegetable stock** (broth)

2 cups (340 g / 12 oz) **quinoa**, rinsed

1 tablespoon **coconut oil**

3 large **onions**, roughly chopped

3 **garlic cloves**, finely chopped

1 **green chile**, plus more to taste, seeded and finely chopped

4 large **tomatoes**, roughly chopped

2 tablespoons **tomato purée** (passata)

1 tablespoon **curry powder**

1 teaspoon **ground turmeric**

1 teaspoon **ground cinnamon**

1 teaspoon **ground cardamom**

1 teaspoon **ground cumin**

½ cup (120 g / 4 oz) canned **red lentils**, drained

salt and freshly ground **black/ white pepper**

cooked **long-grain white rice**, to serve

fresh cilantro (coriander) sprig, to garnish

Bring 2 cups (475 ml / 16 fl oz) of the stock to a boil in a large saucepan. Add the quinoa, then bring the mixture to a simmer over low heat and cook for 14–15 minutes, until the quinoa is cooked. Use a fork to fluff the grains. Set aside.

Heat the coconut oil in a large skillet (frying pan) or wok. Add the onions, garlic, and chile and sauté for 5–6 minutes over medium heat, until lightly golden. Add the tomatoes, tomato purée (passata), curry powder, turmeric, cinnamon, cardamom, and cumin and cook over medium heat, stirring frequently, for 7–8 minutes, until the tomatoes are nicely cooked. If the mixture becomes too dry, add a little water to the pan.

Add the quinoa and lentils to the skillet, along with enough of the remaining stock or water to roughly cover, and simmer over low heat for 20 minutes, until all the ingredients are cooked through.

Season to taste with salt and freshly ground black/white pepper. Serve with rice and garnish with cilantro (coriander).

Rice with Coconut and Papaya

Angola

Serves 4
Preparation time 20 minutes
Cooking time 25 minutes

- 2 cups (400 g / 14 oz) **short-grain white rice**, such as Arborio or Carnaroli
- 2 cups (475 ml / 16 fl oz) **coconut milk**
- 1 teaspoon **ground cinnamon**
- **salt**
- 1 small **papaya**, finely diced
- 2 cups (340 g / 12 oz) diced **pineapple**, to serve

Mix the rice, coconut milk, ⅓ cup (80 ml / 2⅔ fl oz) water, and cinnamon in a large saucepan and season to taste with salt. Bring the mixture to a boil. Reduce the heat to produce a low simmer. Cover the pan and cook over low heat for 20 minutes, until the rice is al dente. If it becomes too dry during cooking, add a little water. Once the rice is cooked, fluff it with a fork, then cover the pan and set aside.

Put half of the papaya in a bowl and mash it with a fork. Add the mashed papaya to the rice and stir to blend, then add the remaining papaya and mix carefully to avoid mashing the diced papaya. Serve warm, with the diced pineapple on top.

Vegetable Paella

Mexico

Serves 4
Preparation time 20 minutes
Cooking time 35 minutes

- 2 tablespoons **olive oil**
- 1 **onion**, chopped
- 1 **green bell pepper**, diced
- 2 **garlic cloves**, finely chopped
- 2 cups (480 g / 1 lb 1 oz) **paella rice**
- 4 cups (950 ml / 32 fl oz) **vegetable broth** (stock)
- 1 cup (200 g / 7 oz) **plum tomatoes**, diced
- 2 **green chiles**, seeded and chopped
- 1 teaspoon **ground turmeric**
- 1 teaspoon **sweet paprika**
- 1 cup (190 g / 6¾ oz) canned **kidney beans**, drained
- 1 cup (140 g / 5 oz) canned or frozen **corn kernels**
- **salt** and freshly ground **black/ white pepper**
- **lemon wedges**, to serve
- crushed **red chili flakes**, to serve

Heat the olive oil in a large skillet (frying pan). Add the onion and stir-fry for 5–6 minutes, until golden brown. Add the green bell pepper and garlic and stir-fry over medium heat for 4–5 minutes, until golden. Add the rice, stock, tomatoes, green chiles, turmeric, and sweet paprika. Bring the mixture to a boil, then reduce the heat to low, cover, and simmer over low heat for 20 minutes.

Stir the kidney beans and corn into the rice mixture, then cover the pan and cook for 5 minutes, until well cooked. Season to taste with salt and freshly ground black/white pepper. Serve with lemon wedges and crushed red chili flakes on the side.

Pasta & Noodles

Five-Spice Stir-Fried Soba Noodles

Malaysia

Serves 4
Preparation time 20 minutes
Cooking time 15 minutes

FOR THE SOBA NOODLES

1 lb 2 oz (500 g) **soba noodles**

1 tablespoon **vegetable oil**

FOR THE SAUCE

½ cup (120 ml / 4 fl oz) fresh **orange juice**

1 tablespoon **cornstarch** (cornflour)

1 teaspoon **five-spice powder**

1 teaspoon crushed **red chili flakes**

2 tablespoons **soy sauce**

2 teaspoons **agave syrup**

FOR THE STIR-FRY

2 tablespoons **olive oil**

1 lb 2 oz (500 g) trimmed and sliced **mushrooms**

2 cups (280 g / 10 oz) **baby carrots**, sliced

1 **onion**, sliced

2 **garlic cloves**, finely chopped

3 cups (520 g / 1 lb 2½ oz) **broccoli florets**

Cook the soba noodles according to the packet instructions. Drain and return to the pan. Stir in the vegetable oil, toss to coat the noodles, then cover the pan and set aside.

To make the sauce, combine the ingredients in a large bowl and whisk until well blended. Set aside.

To make the stir-fry, heat the olive oil in a saucepan over medium heat. Add the mushrooms, carrots, onion, and garlic and stir-fry for 5 minutes, until the onion and garlic are golden. Add the broccoli florets, cover the pan, and cook for 5–6 minutes, stirring occasionally, until the vegetables are crisp-tender. Add the sauce and stir for 3 minutes, or until the sauce has thickened.

Transfer the soba noodles to a serving bowl. Pour the vegetable-sauce mixture over the noodles, toss to combine, and serve immediately.

Lasagna with Mushroom Sauce

Italy

⬠

Serves 4
Preparation time 40 minutes (including cooling)
Cooking time 1 hour 10 minutes

FOR THE MUSHROOM SAUCE

1 tablespoon extra-virgin **olive oil**

1 cup (140 g / 5 oz) chopped **yellow onion**

1 lb 2 oz (500 g) **button mushrooms**, trimmed and sliced

¼ cup (30 g / 1 oz) chopped **fresh parsley**

2 teaspoons ground **rosemary**

1 cup (200 g / 7 oz) canned **plum tomatoes**

FOR THE FILLING

½ cup (30 g / 1 oz) chopped **fresh parsley**

¼ cup (15 g / ½ oz) **fresh basil**

2 cups (60 g / 2 oz) packed **baby spinach**

1 lb (480 g) **firm tofu**

2 cups (250 g / 9 oz) grated **vegan cheddar cheese**

4 tablespoons **rice** or **almond milk**

1 teaspoon **ground nutmeg**

salt and freshly ground **black/ white pepper**

2 lb (900 g) **vegetables**, such as broccoli, artichoke hearts, zucchini (courgette), green beans, asparagus, and yellow and red bell peppers

FOR THE LASAGNA

10 **whole-wheat lasagna sheets**

olive oil, for greasing

salt and freshly ground **black/ white pepper**

2 cups (250 g / 9 oz) grated **vegan cheddar cheese**

To make the mushroom sauce, heat the oil in a large skillet (frying pan). Add the onion and stir-fry over medium heat for 4–5 minutes, until transparent and golden brown. Stir in the mushrooms, parsley, rosemary, and tomatoes. Simmer over medium-low heat for 20 minutes, until well cooked and soft. Set aside.

To make the filling, combine the parsley, basil, and spinach leaves in a food processor and pulse until minced. Add the tofu, cheese, and rice or almond milk. Add the nutmeg and season with salt and freshly ground black/white pepper to taste. Mix well and set aside.

Chop the mixed vegetables, and combine them with the tofu filling in a large bowl. Set aside.

Cook the lasagna sheets according to the instructions on the packet, drain, and pat them dry. Using your fingers or a brush, add a little bit of olive oil on the top of each lasagna sheet and set aside.

To make the lasagna, preheat the oven to 400°F/200°C/Gas Mark 6. Grease a 10 × 13-inch (25 × 33-cm) ovenproof dish with olive oil. Spoon a fine layer of mushroom sauce on the bottom, cover it with a layer of lasagna sheets. Add a third of the vegetables and cover with a third of the mushroom sauce. Sprinkle over a third of the vegan cheddar cheese, cover with another layer of lasagna sheets, and so on, until the lasagna is complete, finishing with the remaining third of cheese. Cover the dish with aluminum foil and bake for 30 minutes. Remove the aluminum foil and bake for another 5 minutes, until the sauce starts to bubble. Let the lasagna cool for 10 minutes before serving.

Macaroni and Roasted Cauliflower Bowl

Morocco

⬠

Serves 4
Preparation time 25 minutes
Cooking time 40 minutes

FOR THE LEMON DRESSING

5 tablespoons fresh **lemon juice**

4 tablespoons **olive oil**

2 tablespoons **agave syrup**

1 tablespoon finely chopped or grated **fresh ginger**

2 **garlic cloves**, finely chopped

1 tablespoon **ground cumin**

1 teaspoon **ground cinnamon**

½ teaspoon **salt**

½ teaspoon freshly ground **black/ white pepper**

FOR THE CAULIFLOWER

2 lb (900 g) **cauliflower florets**

1 lb 2 oz (500 g) **macaroni**

1 cup (220 g / 7¾ oz) slivered **dried apricots**

½ cup (75 g / 3 oz) sliced **green olives**

1 cup (240 g / 8½ oz) crumbled **vegan feta cheese**

¼ cup (30 g / 1 oz) chopped **fresh mint**

Preheat the oven to 400°F/200°C/Gas Mark 6. Line a large baking sheet with parchment (baking) paper or aluminum foil.

To make the lemon dressing, combine the ingredients in a bowl and whisk until well combined.

To make the cauliflower, put it into a large bowl and add 3 tablespoons of the dressing; toss to combine. Reserve the remaining dressing.

Arrange the cauliflower in an even layer on the prepared baking sheet. Roast for 30 minutes, or until golden brown, tossing halfway through.

Meanwhile, cook the pasta according to the instructions on the packet. Drain the pasta, reserving ½ cup (120 ml / 4 fl oz) of the cooking water. Return the pasta to the pan, add the roasted cauliflower, apricots, olives, feta, mint, the reserved pasta water, and the remaining dressing. Toss to combine and serve.

Penne Primavera

Italy

Serves 4
Preparation time 20 minutes
Cooking time 25 minutes

3 tablespoons **olive oil**

1 **onion**, finely chopped

3 **garlic cloves**, chopped

1 teaspoon **coriander seeds**

2 cups (400 g / 14 oz) canned **Puy lentils**, drained

¾ cup (175 ml / 6 fl oz) **dry white wine**, plus more as needed

1 teaspoon **mixed dried Italian herbs**

1 teaspoon **mild curry powder**

1 teaspoon grated **nutmeg**

1 cup (140 g / 5 oz) frozen **green peas**, defrosted

salt and freshly ground **black/ white pepper**

2 cups (475 ml / 16 fl oz) **soy cream**

finely grated zest of 1 **lemon**

1 lb 2 oz (500 g) **penne**

1 tablespoon chopped **fresh parsley**, to garnish

1 teaspoon crushed **pink peppercorns**, to garnish

Heat the oil in a saucepan over medium heat. Add the onion and stir-fry for 5–6 minutes, until golden brown. Add the garlic and coriander seeds and cook for 2 minutes, stirring constantly. Add the lentils and cook for 3–4 minutes. Add the wine, mixed herbs, curry powder, nutmeg, and peas. Reduce the heat to low, cover the pan, and cook for about 10 minutes. Season to taste with salt and freshly ground black/white pepper.

Add the cream to the saucepan 3–4 tablespoons at a time, stirring well between each addition. Leave the pan set on low heat and cook for another 3–4 minutes. If the sauce becomes too thick, add a little wine to loosen it. Stir in half of the zest.

Meanwhile, cook the penne according to the packet instructions until al dente. Rinse under cold running water to stop the cooking, drain completely, and set aside in a large bowl.

When the sauce is ready, mix in the pasta. Transfer to a large serving bowl, garnish with the parsley, the remaining zest, and the pink peppercorns, and serve.

Desserts

Lemon Mousse

Austria

Serves 4
Preparation time 2 hours 45 minutes (including chilling)
Cooking time 15 minutes

2 cups (480 ml / 16 fl oz) **coconut cream**

3 tablespoons **agar-agar**

2 tablespoons **maple syrup**

4 tablespoons fresh **lemon juice**

3 tablespoons **apple sauce**, plus more as needed

2 tablespoons finely grated **lemon zest**

1 teaspoon **vanilla extract**

2 tablespoons **tahini**

a pinch of **salt**

lemon slices, to garnish

Bring 2 cups (480 ml / 16 fl oz) water to a boil in a saucepan. Add the remaining ingredients and reduce the heat to low, then whisk and simmer for 12 minutes, until well blended. Remove the pan from the heat and let cool for 2 hours.

Using a food processor or high-speed blender, process the mixture to the consistency of a smooth and creamy custard. If the mixture is too thick, add more apple sauce. Refrigerate for 30 minutes before serving, garnished with lemon slices.

ChocoBananas

El Salvador

Serves 4
Preparation time 2 hours 20 minutes (including freezing)
Cooking time 10 minutes

6 ripe **bananas**

12½ oz (360 g / 12½ oz) **dark chocolate chips**

2 tablespoons chopped **mixed nuts** (peanuts, pistachio nuts, and almonds)

2 tablespoons **grated coconut**

Line an airtight container with parchment (baking) paper.

Peel the bananas and halve them crosswise. Insert a popsicle stick or a large skewer into the flat end of each banana half, pushing it into the banana about halfway through. Place the bananas in the prepared container and freeze for 2 hours.

Melt the chocolate in a heatproof bowl set over a pan of simmering water, then remove the bowl from the heat.

Place a plastic lidded container in the freezer, but without the lid.

Place the crushed nuts on a plate and the grated coconut on another plate. Dip 1 frozen banana into the melted chocolate and, using a spoon, cover any gaps that remain uncoated. Using a spoon, immediately coat the chocobanana with the crushed nuts and set aside in the freezer. Dip again into the chocolate, this time coating the chocolate-coated banana with grated coconut. Repeat the process, alternating between the 2 coatings, until all the bananas are coated. Act swiftly, as the melted chocolate becomes hard quickly. When done, place the lid on the container of the chocobananas and freeze until ready to serve.

Apple Rice Pudding

Gabon

Serves 4
Preparation time 35 minutes (including chilling)
Cooking time 15 minutes

2 tablespoons **vegetable margarine**

5 tablespoons **maple** or **agave syrup**

1 teaspoon **ground cinnamon**

1 teaspoon **ground nutmeg**

2 **apples**, cored and chopped

2 cups (370 g / 13 oz) **basmati** or other long-grain rice, cooked

½ cup (80 g / 3 oz) **raisins**

2 cups (480 ml / 16 fl oz) **almond milk**

1 cup (80 g / 3 oz) toasted **coconut flakes** (optional)

Heat the vegetable margarine, maple or agave syrup, cinnamon, nutmeg, and apples in a saucepan over medium heat until simmering. Add the rice, raisins, and almond milk. Bring to a simmer and cook over low heat for about 15 minutes, stirring frequently, until the apples are very tender.

Divide the pudding among 4 dessert cups, then let cool for 20 minutes. Decorate with the toasted coconut flakes, if using, and serve.

Banana and Passionfruit Ice Cream

Thailand

Serves 4
Preparation time 12 hours 20 minutes (including freezing)

4 **bananas**
5 tablespoons fresh **coconut water**
2 **passionfruits**
1 tablespoon fresh **lemon juice**
1–2 tablespoons **agave syrup**, to taste
2 tablespoons **coconut flakes**, to garnish

Slice the bananas and place them in a sealed container in the freezer overnight (or longer). Also freeze the bowl or cups in which you will serve the ice cream.

Using a food processor, blend the frozen bananas with the coconut water until smooth. Cut the passionfruits in half, spoon out the pulp, and add it to the banana mixture along with the lemon juice and agave syrup. Pulse for a few seconds until combined.

Transfer to the frozen bowl or cups, garnish with coconut flakes, and serve immediately.

Coconut Panna Cotta with Pineapple

South Africa

Serves 4
Preparation time 20 minutes
Cooking time 30 minutes

FOR THE COCONUT PANNA COTTA

⅔ cup (160 ml / 5 fl oz) **coconut milk**

2 cups (480 ml / 16 fl oz) **soy cream**

1 fresh **vanilla bean** (pod), beans scraped

½ cup (100 g / 3½ oz) **superfine (caster) sugar**

3 teaspoons **agar-agar**

FOR THE PINEAPPLE

½ cup (120 ml / 4 fl oz) **white wine**

½ cup (50 g / 1¾ oz) **superfine (caster) sugar**

1 teaspoon **vanilla extract**

finely grated zest and juice of 1 **lemon**

1 sweet **pineapple**, cored and sliced paper-thin

2 tablespoons **grated coconut**, to decorate

To make the panna cotta, heat the coconut milk, soy cream, vanilla seeds, and sugar in a saucepan. Bring the mixture to a boil, then immediately reduce the heat to low and simmer, stirring continuously, for 6–8 minutes, until the sugar has completely dissolved. Add the agar-agar and stir until it has melted. Pour the custard into 4 ramekins and let cool.

For the pineapple, combine the wine, 1½ cups (360 ml / 12 fl oz) water, sugar, vanilla extract, and lemon juice and zest in a large saucepan and bring the mixture to a boil. Reduce the heat to medium-low, bring the mixture to a simmer, and add the pineapple to the saucepan. Poach gently for 3–4 minutes. Drain the pineapple, reserving the liquid, and set aside to cool. Return the liquid to the saucepan and simmer over medium-low heat for about 15 minutes, until reduced by half and starting to thicken. Let cool.

Arrange equal portions of the pineapple slices on 4 dessert plates. Unmold the panna cottas and position each on top of the pineapple slices. Using a spoon, drizzle 1–2 spoons of the sauce on top. Decorate each panna cotta with ½ tablespoon of grated coconut and serve immediately.

Baked Papaya with Coconut Cream

Haiti

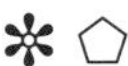

Serves 4
Preparation time 20 minutes
Cooking time 1 hour 30 minutes

2 small **papayas** (not too ripe), halved lengthwise, seeded

½ cup (100 g / 3½ oz) **granulated sugar**

1 cup (240 ml / 8 fl oz) **coconut cream**

⅓ cup (45 g / 1½ oz) **confectioners' (icing) sugar**

1 teaspoon **vanilla extract**

½ cup (120 ml / 4 fl oz) **coconut milk**

Preheat the oven to 375°F/190°C/Gas Mark 5.

Arrange the halved papayas, with the cut sides facing up, in a shallow baking dish. Sprinkle over the granulated sugar and add 4 tablespoons of water to the pan. Bake in the middle of the oven for 1½ hours, until the papayas are tender. Using a spoon, collect the juice of the papaya every half hour. Reserve the juice to sprinkle over the coconut cream at serving time.

Meanwhile, make the coconut cream. Using a food processor or blender, process the coconut cream, confectioners' (icing) sugar, and vanilla extract for 2 minutes, until well blended. Transfer to a bowl and refrigerate until serving.

About 5 minutes before the end of cooking, raise the oven temperature to 400°F/200°C/Gas Mark 6. After 5 minutes, turn off the heat, transfer the papaya to plates, and pour the coconut milk into the cavities of the papayas. Serve on shallow plates, with the chilled thick coconut cream on the side. Sprinkle the reserved papaya juice on top of the chilled thick coconut cream, if desired.

Cantaloupe and Banana Sorbet

France

Serves 4
Preparation time 14 hours 20 minutes (including freezing)

2 lb (900 g) sliced **cantaloupe**
2 **bananas**, sliced
1 tablespoon fresh **lemon juice**
superfine (caster) sugar (optional)
1 tablespoon chopped **fresh mint leaves**, to garnish

Put the cantaloupe and bananas into an airtight container and freeze overnight.

Using a food processor or high-speed blender, process the frozen fruits and lemon juice until smooth. Taste and adjust the sweetness by adding superfine (caster) sugar, if needed. Place the fruit purée in an airtight container and freeze for 2 hours.

Scoop the sorbet into bowls, garnish with chopped mint leaves, and serve.

ZEROLL

Lemon-Cinnamon Rice Milk

Central African Republic

Serves 4
Preparation time 30 minutes
Cooking time 20 minutes

1¼ cups (260 g / 9 oz) **long-grain white rice**

1 **cinnamon stick**

finely grated zest of 1 **lemon**

a pinch of **salt**

4 cups (960 ml / 32½ fl oz) **coconut milk**

1 cup (200 g / 7 oz) **granulated sugar**

1 teaspoon **ground cinnamon**, to garnish

Place the rice in a pot, and add the cinnamon, half of the zest, and salt. Cook the rice according to the packet instructions until cooked through. Add the coconut milk, sugar, and remaining lemon zest to the pan. Bring to a boil, then immediately reduce the heat to medium-low and simmer for about 15 minutes, until the mixture is very creamy. Remove the pan from the stove and transfer to serving bowls. Dust with cinnamon and serve warm.

Blood Orange Crème Brûlée

Malawi

Serves 4
Preparation time 1 hour 15 minutes (including chilling)
Cooking time 40 minutes

1 **vanilla bean** (pod), seeds scraped
1 cup (240 ml / 8 fl oz) **soy cream**
¼ cup (60 ml / 2 fl oz) **almond milk**
2 tablespoons **egg replacer**, mixed with 4 tablespoons **warm water**
¼ cup (50 g / 1¾ oz) **superfine (caster) sugar,** plus 2 tablespoons
4 tablespoons fresh **orange juice**
1 tablespoon finely grated **orange zest**

Preheat the oven to 300°F/150°C/Gas Mark 2.

Combine the vanilla seeds, soy cream, and almond milk in a saucepan and stir well. Bring the mixture to a boil over medium heat, then immediately reduce the heat to low and simmer for 6 minutes, whisking occasionally, until the mixture thickens.

Combine the egg replacer with the ¼ cup (50 g / 1¾ oz) superfine (caster) sugar in a large bowl, then gradually pour in the thickened cream, whisking constantly. Mix in the orange juice and zest.

Pour the mixture into 4 ramekins and place them in a large baking pan. Pour boiling water into the baking pan so that it reaches halfway up the sides of the ramekins. Transfer to the oven and bake for 35 minutes. Remove the ramekins from the oven and the water bath and refrigerate for 1 hour before serving.

Just before serving, sprinkle ½ tablespoon sugar on top of each ramekin and, using a kitchen blowtorch, caramelize the sugar until golden brown.

Cranberry Pudding

Lithuania

Serves 4
Preparation time 1 hour 30 minutes (including cooling and chilling)
Cooking time 30 minutes

2 cups (480 g / 1 lb 1 oz) fresh **cranberries**

2 **cinnamon sticks**

4 whole **cloves**

1 cup (200 g / 7 oz) **superfine (caster) sugar**

1 cup (125 g / 4½ oz) **cornstarch** (cornflour)

Put the cranberries into a saucepan. Pour in enough water to cover the berries, and add the cinnamon and cloves. Bring the water to a boil, then reduce the heat to medium-low and simmer for 10–12 minutes, until the cranberries begin to pop. Remove the pan from the heat and let cool for 20 minutes. Discard the cinnamon and cloves.

Using a food processor or a high-speed blender, process the cranberries for 2–3 minutes until very smooth. Add the sugar and blend for 2–3 minutes, until the sugar has been completely incorporated.

Transfer the mixture to a saucepan. Add half of the cranberry mixture and the cornstarch (cornflour), stirring constantly until everything is well blended. Stir in the remaining cranberry mixture, then bring everything to a simmer, stirring frequently. Cook over medium-low heat for about 10 minutes, until the mixture thickens.

Transfer the cranberry pudding to 4 individual dishes and let cool for 20 minutes. Refrigerate for 30 minutes before serving.

Chocolate Truffles

Sweden

Makes 24–30 truffles
Preparation time 1 hour 25 minutes (including chilling)
Cooking time 10 minutes

½ cup (120 g / 4 oz) **vegetable margarine**

1 teaspoon **vanilla extract**

½ cup (100 g / 3½ oz) **superfine (caster) sugar**

3 cups (270 g / 9½ oz) quick-cooking **oats**

⅓ cup (180 g / 6 oz) **dark chocolate chips**

3 tablespoons **cognac** or **brandy**

unsweetened **cocoa powder**, for rolling

Mix the vegetable margarine, vanilla, sugar, and oats in a bowl until well blended.

Melt the chocolate in a heatproof bowl set over a saucepan of simmering water. Mix the melted chocolate into the vegetable margarine–oat mixture. Add the cognac or brandy and stir to combine.

Spread the cocoa powder on a plate. Using your hands, take walnut-size pieces of the mixture and roll them into balls, then roll them in the cocoa powder. This mixture should yield 24–30 chocolate truffles. Refrigerate for 1 hour before serving.

Chocolate-Cherry and Pistachio Biscotti

South Africa

Serves 4
Preparation time 45 minutes (including cooling)
Cooking time 1 hour 15 minutes

- 2 cups (250 g / 9 oz) **all-purpose (plain) flour**, plus extra for dusting
- 2 tablespoons **canola (rapeseed) oil**
- ½ cup (50 g / 1¾ oz) unsweetened **cocoa powder**
- ½ cup (60 g / 2 oz) **confectioners' (icing) sugar**
- 1 teaspoon **baking powder**
- a pinch of **salt**
- 2 tablespoons **egg replacer**, mixed with 4 tablespoons **warm water**
- 1 **vanilla bean** (pod), seeds scraped
- 1 tablespoon finely grated **orange zest**
- 1 cup (140 g / 5 oz) toasted **pistachio nuts**, crushed
- ½ cup (120 g / 4 oz) **cherries**, halved and pitted (stoned)
- ¼ cup (60 ml / 2 fl oz) **almond milk**, plus more as needed

Preheat the oven to 350°F/180°C/Gas Mark 4. Dust a baking sheet with all-purpose (plain) flour.

Combine the flour, oil, cocoa powder, confectioners' (icing) sugar, baking powder, salt, and egg replacer in a bowl. Add the vanilla seeds and orange zest and stir until well combined. Add the nuts, cherries, and almond milk. Using your hands, knead together to form a soft dough. If the dough is too dry, add more almond milk.

Dust your hands with flour and dust your work surface, too. Using your hands, roll the dough into a log. Transfer it to the prepared baking sheet and bake for 30 minutes, until firm. Transfer the log to a wire rack.

Reduce the oven heat to 275°F/140°C/Gas Mark 1.

Cut the log into slices. Place the slices flat on the same baking sheet and bake for about 45 minutes, until the biscotti are dry and crisped up. Let cool on a wire rack for 15 minutes before serving.

Chocolate-Mint Macarons

New Zealand

Serves 4
Preparation time 1 hour 50 minutes (including resting and chilling)
Cooking time 20 minutes

FOR THE MACARONS

2 cups (260 g / 9 oz) **ground almonds**

2 cups (240 g / 8½ oz) **confectioners' (icing) sugar**

5 tablespoons **liquid from canned chickpeas**

1 teaspoon **xanthan gum**

⅓ cup (65 g / 2 oz) **superfine (caster) sugar**

1 teaspoon **peppermint extract**

FOR THE CHOCOLATE CREAM

1⅓ cups (300 g / 10½ oz) **dark chocolate chips**

4 tablespoons **coconut cream**

To make the macarons, sift the ground almonds and confectioners' (icing) sugar into a bowl and set aside. Line a baking sheet with parchment (baking) paper.

Using a food processor or hand-held electric mixer, whisk the chickpea juice on a high-speed setting until it begins to thicken, then slowly sprinkle in the xanthan gum. Once soft peaks start to form, slowly whisk in the superfine (caster) sugar 1 teaspoon at a time. Add the peppermint extract and continue to whisk for 1 minute. Gradually whisk the ground almond mixture into the meringue until well combined and firm. Transfer the mixture to a pastry (piping) bag.

Pipe the meringue onto the parchment paper in 1-inch (2.5 cm) diameter circles. Flatten the little peaks on the tops of the macarons so that they are flat. Set aside for 30 minutes. Preheat the oven to 275°F/140°C/Gas Mark 1.

Bake the macarons for 15 minutes, then leave the oven door open for 2 minutes to let out the heat. Close the oven door and bake for another 5 minutes, until the macarons are firm. Let cool completely on the baking sheet.

To make the chocolate cream, melt the chocolate and coconut cream together in a saucepan over medium heat. Once the chocolate has melted, transfer to a container and refrigerate for 45 minutes.

To assemble the macarons, place 1½ teaspoons of chocolate cream on the flat surface of half of the macarons, and sandwich with the remaining macarons, pressing gently until the cream fills the space between the macarons completely. Repeat with the remaining macarons and chocolate sauce. Serve immediately.

Cakes & Pies

Salty Caramel Cake

Austria

Makes 1 (9-inch/23 cm) cake
Preparation time 45 minutes (including cooling)
Cooking time 30 minutes

vegetable margarine, for greasing

½ cup (65 g / 2 oz) plus 1 tablespoon **whole-wheat (wholemeal) flour**

6 tablespoons unsweetened **cocoa powder**

2 teaspoons **baking powder**

3 tablespoons **vegetable oil**

3 tablespoons **maple syrup**

1 tablespoon **vanilla sugar**

6 tablespoons **almond butter**

¼ teaspoon **salt**, plus extra flaky sea salt to garnish

1 cup (240 ml / 8 fl oz) **almond milk**

3 tablespoons **dark chocolate chips**

Preheat the oven to 350°F/180°C/Gas Mark 4. Grease a 9-inch (23 cm) round cake pan with vegetable margarine.

Mix the flour, cocoa powder, and baking powder in a bowl. Set aside.

To make the caramel, combine the oil, maple syrup, vanilla sugar, almond butter, and salt in a saucepan. Heat over medium heat, stirring constantly, for 6–7 minutes, until the caramel is bubbling and smooth. Set aside for 10 minutes.

Mix half the almond butter mixture with the flour mixture. Add the almond milk and chocolate and stir to combine. Pour the batter into the prepared cake pan. Drizzle the remaining almond butter mixture over the top. Bake for about 25 minutes, or until a skewer inserted in the center of the cake comes out clean. Set aside to cool on a wire rack for 15 minutes before serving, garnished with a little flaky sea salt.

Carrot Cake with Cream Cheese Frosting

United States

Makes 1 (9-inch/23 cm) cake
Preparation time 55 minutes (including chilling)
Cooking time 45 minutes

FOR THE CAKE

vegetable margarine, for greasing

1 cup (125 g / 4½ oz) **all-purpose (plain) flour**

1 cup (200 g / 7 oz) **superfine (caster) sugar**

1 teaspoon **ground cinnamon**

1 teaspoon **baking soda** (bicarbonate of soda)

a pinch of **salt**

2 tablespoons **coconut flakes**

2 cups (260 g / 9 oz) grated **carrots**, plus extra to decorate

1½ cups (135 g / 4¾ oz) **walnuts**, chopped, plus extra to decorate

½ cup (120 ml / 4 fl oz) **vegetable oil**

2 tablespoons **egg replacer**, mixed in 4 tablespoons **warm water**

1 teaspoon **vanilla extract**

1 cup (170 g / 6 oz) chopped fresh sweet **pineapple,** plus extra to decorate

FOR THE FROSTING (ICING)

½ cup (120 g / 4 oz) **vegan cream cheese**

¼ cup (60 g / 2 oz) **vegetable margarine**

½ cup (60 g / 2 oz) **confectioners' (icing) sugar**

Preheat the oven to 350°F/180°C/Gas Mark 4. Grease a 9-inch (23 cm) round springform pan with vegetable margarine.

To make the cake batter, mix the flour, sugar, cinnamon, baking soda (bicarbonate of soda), and salt in a large bowl. Stir in the coconut flakes, carrots, and nuts, then the oil, egg replacer, vanilla, and pineapple and mix well to form a smooth, lump-free batter. Spread the batter in the prepared cake pan and bake for 45 minutes, until the cake is baked through but still spongy. Let cool, then remove from the pan.

To make the frosting, whisk the cream cheese and vegetable margarine with the sugar in a bowl until combined and fluffy. Using a silicone spatula, spread the frosting across the top surface of the cake. Refrigerate the cake for 30 minutes, then decorate with grated carrot, chopped walnuts, and chopped pineapple before serving.

Pomegranate and Semolina Cakes

Spain

Serves 4
Preparation time 55 minutes (including cooling)
Cooking time 20 minutes

1 cup (240 ml / 8 fl oz) **pomegranate juice**

1 cup (200 g / 7 oz) **superfine (caster) sugar**

2 cups (280 g / 10 oz) **semolina flour**

2 tablespoons **rosewater**

1 cup (135 g / 4¾ oz) **ground almonds**

2 tablespoons **confectioners' (icing) sugar**

Combine the pomegranate juice and superfine (caster) sugar in a saucepan set over medium-low heat. Stir until the sugar has dissolved, then bring to a boil. Immediately remove the pan from the heat and let cool for 15 minutes.

Return the pan to the stove and bring the mixture to a low simmer. Stir in the semolina, then the rosewater, and simmer gently over medium-low heat for 10 minutes. Add the ground almonds, mix well, and let cool for 20 minutes.

When cool enough to handle with your hands, roll the mixture into small, walnut-size balls and set aside.

Put the confectioners' (icing) sugar into a bowl. Roll the semolina balls in the sugar to coat completely before serving.

Matcha, Chocolate, and Date Cake

United States

Makes 1 (8 × 4-inch/20 × 10 cm) cake
Preparation time 4 hours 40 minutes (including chilling)

1½ cups (135 g / 4¾ oz) **walnuts**

½ cup (90 g / 3¼ oz) **Medjool dates**

2 tablespoons **ground almonds**

3 tablespoons unsweetened **cocoa powder**, divided

2½ teaspoons **matcha powder**, divided

2 tablespoons **maple syrup**

1 teaspoon **vanilla extract**

½ cup (90 g / 3¼ oz) **dark chocolate chips**, melted

1 tablespoon **ground ginger**

Line an 8 × 4-inch (20 × 10 cm) cake pan with parchment (baking) paper.

Using a food processor, pulse the walnuts a couple of times, then add the dates and pulse until the mixture is broken down and sticky. Add the ground almonds, 2 tablespoons of the cocoa powder, 1½ teaspoons of the matcha, the maple syrup, vanilla, and melted chocolate. Pulse again until all the ingredients are well incorporated and the mixture is smooth. Transfer the mixture to a large bowl, add the ginger, and mix well to combine.

Spoon the mixture into the prepared cake pan and press it into the bottom in a thick layer. Use a rubber spatula to smooth out the top into a flat surface. Cover the pan with plastic wrap (clingfilm) and refrigerate for 3–4 hours.

To serve, cut the block into 1-inch (2.5 cm) squares. Dust the squares with the remaining cocoa and matcha powders just before serving.

Orange-Ginger Cheesecake

United States

Makes 1 (8-inch/20 cm) cake
Preparation time 4 hours 20 minutes (including chilling and cooling)
Cooking time 1 hour 30 minutes

FOR THE BASE

3 cups (375 g / 13¼ oz) **vegan ginger snaps**

⅓ cup (80 ml / 2¾ fl oz) melted **vegetable margarine**

FOR THE CHEESECAKE FILLING

3 cups (720 g / 1 lb 9 oz) **vegan cream cheese**, at room temperature

1 cup (240 g / 8½ oz) **vegan sour cream**, at room temperature

½ cup (100 g / 3½ oz) **superfine (caster) sugar**

4 tablespoons **egg replacer**, mixed with 8 tablespoons **warm water**

grated zest and juice of 1 **orange**

FOR THE TOPPING

1 cup (200 g / 7 oz) **superfine (caster) sugar**

2 tablespoons grated **fresh ginger**

4 **oranges**, peeled and membranes trimmed, segments divided

Preheat the oven to 250°F/130°C/Gas Mark ½.

To make the base, using a food processor fitted with a blade, pulse the ginger snaps to fine crumbs. Transfer to a bowl and mix in the melted vegetable margarine until combined. Press the mixture into the bottom of an 8-inch (20 cm) springform cake pan. Set aside in a freezer for 1 hour.

To make the cheesecake filling, whisk together the ingredients in a bowl until smooth. Taste and adjust the sweetness as needed. Pour the filling over the base. Bake for 1½ hours, until the filling is set. Let cool on a wire rack for 30 minutes.

To make the topping, put the sugar and ½ cup (120 ml / 4 fl oz) water in a saucepan and heat gently over medium-low heat until the sugar has dissolved. Bring to a boil, then immediately reduce the heat to low and simmer for 3 minutes. Remove the pan from the heat, add the ginger and orange segments, and let cool for 20 minutes.

Arrange the orange segments over the cheesecake and brush with the ginger topping. Refrigerate for 2 hours before serving.

Lime Cheesecake (raw)

French Polynesia

Makes 1 (9-inch/23 cm) cake
Preparation time 3 hours 25 minutes (including chilling)

FOR THE BASE

vegetable oil, for greasing

2 cups (240 g / 8½ oz) raw **cashews**, soaked in water overnight and drained

1 cup (90 g / 3¼ oz) **coconut flakes**

½ cup (120 g / 4 oz) pitted (stoned) **dates**

½ cup (50 g / 1¾ oz) raw **cacao nibs**

a pinch of **salt**

FOR THE FILLING

1 large **Hass avocado**, peeled and pitted (stoned)

1½ cups (360 g / 12½ oz) **cashews**, soaked in water for at least 2 hours and drained

½ cup (120 ml / 4 fl oz) melted **coconut oil**

¼ cup (60 ml / 2 fl oz) fresh **lime juice**

½ cup (120 ml / 4 fl oz) **maple** or **agave syrup**

1 teaspoon **vanilla extract**

a pinch of **sea salt**

1 tablespoon finely grated **lime zest**, to garnish

Grease a 9-inch (23 cm) springform cake pan with vegetable oil. To make the base, using a food processor, pulse the cashews, coconut flakes, pitted (stoned) dates, cacao nibs, and salt a couple of times until they are mixed and broken down. Spoon the mixture evenly over the bottom of the prepared cake pan. Press with your fingers to make a firm base. Set aside in the refrigerator.

To make the filling, using a food processor or a high-speed blender, combine all the ingredients and process until smooth and creamy. Spread the filling over the base and, using a rubber spatula, create a smooth surface.

Chill the pie in the freezer for 1 hour, then transfer to the refrigerator for 2 hours before garnishing with lime zest and serving.

Raspberry Pie

England

Makes 1 (9-inch/23 cm) pie
Preparation time 1 hour 35 minutes (including chilling)

FOR THE CRUST

1 tablespoon **coconut oil**

8 **Medjool dates**, pitted (stoned)

1½ cups (135 g / 4¾ oz) **walnuts**

1 tablespoon **agave** or **maple syrup**

a pinch of **salt**

FOR THE FILLING

½ cup (120 g / 4 oz) raw **cashews**, soaked in water overnight and drained

1 tablespoon **agave syrup**

1 teaspoon **vanilla extract**

1 tablespoon fresh **lemon juice**

1 cup (125 g / 4½ oz) **raspberries**, divided

1 tablespoon **confectioners' (icing) sugar**, for dusting (optional)

To make the crust, using a food processor, pulse the ingredients until they form sticky crumbs. Spoon the crumbs into a 9-inch (23 cm) round tart pan and press them into the bottom and sides. Set aside in the freezer.

To make the filling, using a food processor or high-speed blender, process the drained cashews, agave, vanilla extract, lemon juice, and ¼ cup (30 g / 1 oz) of the raspberries until smooth and creamy. Pour the filling onto the base and spread it evenly across the surface. Top with the remaining raspberries, pressing them carefully into the cashew cream. Refrigerate for 1 hour, then dust with confectioners' (icing) sugar over the raspberries, if using, and serve.

Vegan Pantry

Vegan Pantry

The following items are useful to keep in your pantry if you are looking to follow a vegan diet. Choose your fruits and vegetables seasonally, and you will always have a good selection on hand.

FRESH FRUITS AND VEGETABLES

- [ ] Apples
- [ ] Avocados
- [ ] Bean sprouts
- [ ] Beets (Beetroot)
- [ ] Bell peppers
- [ ] Broccoli
- [ ] Cabbage
- [ ] Carrots
- [ ] Cauliflower
- [ ] Celery
- [ ] Chiles
- [ ] Cucumber
- [ ] Daikon Radish
- [ ] Eggplants (aubergines)
- [ ] Garlic
- [ ] Ginger
- [ ] Herbs
- [ ] Kale and other hearty greens
- [ ] Leeks
- [ ] Lemons
- [ ] Lettuce
- [ ] Limes
- [ ] Mango
- [ ] Mushrooms
- [ ] Onions
- [ ] Pineapple
- [ ] Potatoes
- [ ] Pumpkin
- [ ] Raspberries
- [ ] Scallions (spring onions)
- [ ] Spinach

- [ ] Squash
- [ ] Sweet Potatoes
- [ ] Tomatoes
- [ ] Zucchini (courgette)

GRAINS

- [ ] Barley
- [ ] Buckwheat
- [ ] Bulgur
- [ ] Couscous
- [ ] Farro
- [ ] Kamut
- [ ] Millet
- [ ] Oats
- [ ] Quinoa
- [ ] Rice: basmati, black, brown, jasmine, red, risotto, sticky, white, wild
- [ ] Spelt
- [ ] Wheatberries

PASTA AND NOODLES

- [ ] Bean thread noodles
- [ ] Rice noodles
- [ ] Soba
- [ ] Udon
- [ ] Various dry pastas

FLOURS

- [ ] All-purpose (plain) flour
- [ ] Almond meal or almond flour
- [ ] Brown rice flour
- [ ] Buckwheat flour
- [ ] Chickpea flour
- [ ] Cornmeal
- [ ] Kamut flour
- [ ] Oat flour
- [ ] Semolina flour
- [ ] Spelt flour
- [ ] Whole wheat (whole meal) pastry flour

BEANS AND LEGUMES

- [ ] Chickpeas: canned, dry
- [ ] Lentils: black beluga, green, Puy, red, yellow
- [ ] Tempeh
- [ ] Tofu
- [ ] Beans: black beans, black-eyed peas, navy beans, edamame, red kidney beans, split peas

RAW NUTS AND SEEDS

- [ ] Almonds
- [ ] Cashews
- [ ] Macadamia
- [ ] Peanuts
- [ ] Pecans
- [ ] Pine nuts
- [ ] Seeds: chia, hemp, pumpkin, sesame, sunflower, whole flax
- [ ] Walnuts

DRIED FRUITS AND VEGETABLES

- [ ] Apricots
- [ ] Cherries
- [ ] Cranberries
- [ ] Dates
- [ ] Mangos
- [ ] Mushrooms
- [ ] Nori
- [ ] Prunes
- [ ] Raisins

VINEGARS

- [ ] Balsamic vinegar
- [ ] Raw apple cider vinegar
- [ ] Red wine vinegar
- [ ] Rice vinegar

SWEETENERS

- [ ] Medjool dates
- [ ] Molasses
- [ ] Pure maple syrup
- [ ] Raw agave syrup
- [ ] Raw coconut sugar
- [ ] Sucanat sugar
- [ ] Unrefined cane sugar
- [ ] Unrefined dark brown sugar

CHOCOLATE

- [ ] Dark chocolate: sweetened, unsweetened
- [ ] Cacao nibs

SUNDRIES AND CONDIMENTS

- [ ] Almond milk
- [ ] Canned beans
- [ ] Canned tomatoes
- [ ] Capers
- [ ] Cocoa butter
- [ ] Coconut milk: full-fat, light
- [ ] Coconut cream
- [ ] Gochugaru
- [ ] Ground almonds
- [ ] Harissa
- [ ] Ketchup
- [ ] Matzo meal
- [ ] Mustard
- [ ] Nut and seed butters: raw almond butter, roasted natural peanut butter
- [ ] Nutritional yeast
- [ ] Oil: canola (rapeseed), sesame, vegetable
- [ ] Olives
- [ ] Pickles
- [ ] Preserved lemons
- [ ] Sambal oelek
- [ ] Soy milk
- [ ] Soy sauce
- [ ] Soy cream
- [ ] Sriracha
- [ ] Tahini
- [ ] Tamari
- [ ] Tomato paste (purée)
- [ ] Tomato purée (passata)
- [ ] Vegan cheeses
- [ ] Vegan mayonnaise
- [ ] Vegetable broth (stock)
- [ ] Unsweetened applesauce

SPICES

- [ ] Allspice
- [ ] Anise seed
- [ ] Bay leaves
- [ ] Caraway
- [ ] Cayenne
- [ ] Celery seed
- [ ] Chili powder
- [ ] Chinese five-spice blend
- [ ] Cinnamon
- [ ] Cream of tartar
- [ ] Cumin
- [ ] Curry
- [ ] Dry mustard
- [ ] Garam masala
- [ ] Garlic powder
- [ ] Ground cardamom
- [ ] Ground cloves
- [ ] Ground coriander seed
- [ ] Ground ginger
- [ ] Ground turmeric
- [ ] Mustard seed: black, yellow
- [ ] Nutmeg
- [ ] Oregano
- [ ] Paprika: hot, smoked, sweet
- [ ] Peppercorns: black, pink, white
- [ ] Red pepper flakes
- [ ] Salt: coarse sea, fine sea, flaky, kosher
- [ ] Star anise

Index

Index

P

Q

R

S

Recipe Notes

All herbs are fresh, unless otherwise specified.

Individual vegetables and fruits, such as onions and apples, are assumed to be medium, unless otherwise specified.

All salt is fine sea salt, unless otherwise specified.

Exercise a high level of caution when following recipes involving any potentially hazardous activity, including the use of high temperatures, open flames, and when deep-frying. In particular, when deep-frying add food carefully to avoid splashing, wear long sleeves, and never leave the pan unattended.

Cooking times are for guidance only. If using a fan (convection) oven, follow the manufacturer's instructions concerning the oven temperatures.

All herbs, shoots, flowers, and leaves should be picked fresh from a clean source. Do exercise caution when foraging for ingredients, which should only be eaten if an expert has deemed them safe to eat. In particular, do not gather wild mushrooms yourself before seeking the advice of an expert who has confirmed their suitability for human consumption. As some species of mushrooms have been known to cause allergic reaction and illness, do take extra care when cooking and eating mushrooms and do seek immediate medical help if you experience a reaction after preparing or eating them.

Exercise caution when making fermented products, ensuring all equipment is spotlessly clean, and seek expert advice if in any doubt.

When no quantity is specified, for example of oils, salts, and herbs used for finishing dishes, quantities are discretionary and flexible.

All spoon and cup measurements are level, unless otherwise stated. 1 teaspoon = 5 ml; 1 tablespoon = 15 ml. Australian standard tablespoons are 20 ml, so Australian readers are advised to use 3 teaspoons in place of 1 tablespoon when measuring small quantities.

Cup, metric, and imperial measurements are used in this book. Follow one set of measurements throughout, not a mixture, as they are not interchangeable.

Author Biography

Jean-Christian Jury was a renowned vegan and raw-food chef from Toulouse, France. In 2008, he opened La Mano Verde in Berlin, Germany, his first vegan restaurant, and received praise from *Saveur* and *Rodale's Organic Life*, as well as many other international publications. He was the author of two books on vegan cuisine, including the critically acclaimed *Vegan: The Cookbook*, published by Phaidon in 2017.

Phaidon Press Limited
2 Cooperage Yard
London E15 2QR

Phaidon Press Inc.
111 Broadway
New York, NY 10006

Phaidon SARL
55, rue Traversière
75012 Paris

phaidon.com

First published 2026

ISBN 978 1 83729 157 1

The recipes in this book are from *Vegan: The Cookbook*. The first English edition of *Vegan: The Cookbook* was published by Phaidon in 2017.

A CIP catalogue record for this book is available from the British Library and the Library of Congress.

Commissioning Editor: Emily Takoudes
Project Editor: Rachel Malig
Production Controller: Adela Cory
Design: Gabrielle Guy
Photography: Sidney Bensimon

Printed in China

The publishers would like to thank Hilary Bird, Julia Hasting, João Mota, Ellie Smith, Tracey Smith, and Kathy Steer for their contributions to the book.